# CHANGING VOCATIONAL EDUCATION AND TRAINING

Many developed and developing nations are looking to their vocational education and training (VET) systems to provide a response to changes in the global economy. Some countries are proactive with regard to these changes, adopting long-term strategies that could benefit their economies. These strategies include coordinating economic, industrial and VET policies and achieving consensus among the major stakeholders in the system.

*Changing Vocational Education and Training* attempts to identify how consensus on VET policy is sought in a number of countries, where interesting models of response have occurred. Based on the findings of a seminar organised by the University of Strathclyde and the Advisory Scottish Council for Education and Training Targets in 1996, the focus is on the principles of stakeholding, consensus, participation and democracy applied to policy formulation and implementation in VET. The international case studies, presented and discussed by expert from eight nations, provide sound examples of practical strategies whic  e been successfully implemented and will be of interest to p  makers, practitioners and academics.

**Ian Finlay** teaches at the Scottish School of Further Education at the University of Strathclyde. He is also editor of *A Journal for Further and Higher Education in Scotland*.

**Stuart Niven** has just retired from the post of Director of the Scottish School of Further Education. He is President Emeritus of the International Vocational Education and Training Association.

**Stephanie Young** is Director of Lifelong Learning with Glasgow Development Agency.

# ILLUSTRATIONS

## Figures

CONTENTS

# CONTENTS

First published 1998
by Routledge
11 New Fetter Lane, London EC4P 4EE

Simultaneously published in the USA and Canada
by Routledge
29 West 35th Street, New York, NY 10001

Typeset in Garamond by Routledge
Printed and bound in Great Britain by Clays Ltd, St Ives PLC

*British Library Cataloguing in Publication Data*
A catalogue record for this book is available from the British Library

*Library of Congress Cataloging in Publication Data*
Changing vocational education and training: an international comparative
perspective / edited by Ian Finlay, Stuart Niven, and Stephanie Young.
p. cm.
Includes bibliographical references and index.
1. Vocational education – Cross-cultural studies. 2. Occupational training –
Cross-cultural studies. 3. Education and State – Cross-cultural studies. 4.
Educational change – Cross-cultural studies.
I. Finlay, Ian, 1952– . II. Niven, Stuart. III. Young, Stephanie.
LC1043.C52 1998
370.11'3–dc21          98–20946
CIP

ISBN 0–415–18142–9 (hbk)
ISBN 0–415–18143–7 (pbk)

# CHANGING VOCATIONAL EDUCATION AND TRAINING

An international comparative perspective

*Edited by Ian Finlay, Stuart Niven and Stephanie Young*

London and New York

## Tables

# NOTES ON CONTRIBUTORS

**Ian Bellis** is Professor of Human Resource Development at Rand Afrikaans University and leads a human resource development consultancy. Educated at Rhodes and Oxford Universities, he has been involved in education and human resources for thirty years. He has been closely involved in the change process in South Africa by facilitating the National Training Board Committee that formulated the National Qualifications Framework.

**Betsy Brand** is President of Workforce Futures Inc., a consultancy organisation specialising in vocational education and training policy. She has worked on federal and state projects in the United States and also on international projects. She is a former Assistant Secretary for Vocational and Adult Education in the US Department of Education of the Bush administration where she was responsible for VET policy. She has published a range of chapters and articles on vocational education.

**Willi Brand** is a Professor in the Institute of Vocational Education at the University of Hamburg. He has been a visiting lecturer to Jordanhill College of Education and has published several articles on the German VET system.

**John Fairley** holds the Chair of Public Policy at the Robert Gordon University, Aberdeen. He has published widely on the education and training system in the United Kingdom including an entry in the International Encyclopaedia of Education. He has provided consultancy to local government and to development agencies in the UK and internationally.

**Ian Finlay** teaches in the Scottish School of Further Education at the University of Strathclyde. He has degrees in economics and in education. He has taught in further and higher education and spent two years as a freelance training consultant. He has researched and published widely in the fields of comparative education, and education and training policy. He is editor of *A Journal for Further and Higher Education in Scotland*.

**Jim Gleeson** teaches in the Department of Second Level Education in the University of Limerick. He has been closely involved in the development of vocational curricula in Ireland and has also conducted research into vocational training for the European Union.

**Stuart Niven** has recently retired from the post of Director of the Scottish School of Further Education. He is President Emeritus of the International Vocational Education and Training Association. He has conducted consultancy on technical and vocational education in Austria, Nepal, Turkey and the United States, and is a regular contributor to international conferences on vocational education and training. Recent publications include a survey of VET systems and guidelines for the international accreditation of VET systems, institutions and programmes.

**Olli Räty** is Director of the Further Education Centre for Vocational Institutes and Administration in Tampere, Finland. He is a senior advisor to the Finnish government on VET and has also conducted consultancy assignments internationally. In recent years he has had a leading role in organising European seminars on aspects of VET for the Council of Europe.

**Dar-chin Rau** is Director of the Technological and Vocational Education Research Centre in the National Taiwan Normal University, one of the leading institutions in the field of human resource development in East Asia. He has published widely on VET matters and has made important contributions at international conferences.

**Johnny Sung** is a lecturer at the Centre for Labour Market Studies at the University of Leicester. He specialises in the VET and human resource development policies and practices of countries in South East Asia, where he spends part of his time teaching. He is joint editor of *Vocational Education and Training in the Federal Republic of Germany, France Japan, Singapore and the United States* published by the Centre for Labour Market Studies.

**Stephanie Young** is Director of Lifelong Learning with Glasgow Development Agency. Her career has spanned both the public and private sectors. She has been involved in business, economic and human resource development. Her advice is regularly sought by political leaders. Her published work includes policy documents and newspaper articles on education and training.

# ACKNOWLEDGEMENTS

We would like to acknowledge the support of the Advisory Scottish Council for Education and Training Targets who funded the initial seminar which gave us the idea and some material for this book. We would also like to thank the University of Strathclyde from which we also received support, both from the institution and from individuals. The Faculty of Education's research fund and supportive framework helped Ian and Stuart with time to do the necessary work. The writers' group of the university led by Gilbert Mackay and Rowena Murray helped Ian to get going. Ken McLaren and Moira Ferry helped to get work submitted from authors all over the world, making different computer formats into a common format. Ian and Stuart were ably assisted by excellent secretaries in Moira Ferry and Sandra Little, and all three of us appreciated Sandra Littlejohn's help in organising the initial seminar. Ian would like to thank his friends, both staff and students of the Scottish School of Further Education over the past seven years, who have helped him to clarify his thoughts on some of the issues covered in this book. Thanks also to Kath Finlay for her help with proof reading. Finally thanks to Helen Fairlie of Routledge for her support and friendship over the years. The book has benefited from the help of all the people listed above, but any mistakes remain our responsibility.

Ian Finlay
Stuart Niven
Stephanie Young

# INTRODUCTION

*Stephanie Young*

Policies for vocational education are linked to national aspirations and achievements in economic growth. Thus they are influenced by past successes and failures as well as future hopes. There is an acknowledged strong statistical relationship between educational attainment and economic growth but the relationship is not the simple one of cause and effect. Although knowledge of the precise details of the connection remain imperfect, no political system nowadays can maintain itself long without giving due recognition to the notion that the provision of education services enriches the quality and capacity of labour and in the process improves employability and flexibility and thus the rationality of the labour market.

How the state organises this enrichment process varies throughout the world. The UK established a responsibility for general education in the last quarter of the nineteenth century but it was only in the 1960s that it extended its responsibility to include vocational training. The Singapore government also instituted vocational education policies during the 1960s but with a background colonial history, exclusion from the Federation of Malaysia in 1965, multiple ethnic groups and an under-developed economy the shape of government intervention was distinctly different.

The intervention of the state in vocational education reflects its concern over the supply of labour within the typology of the reigning industrial policy. Russia before 1989 essentially typifies the command model where centralised, coercive state planning organises the vast bulk of economic activity. At the other end of the continuum is the neo-liberal model epitomised by the triumphalist economics of Reagan and Thatcher under whom state interference and intervention were radically attenuated and, on the basis of its alleged instrumental efficiency, the competitive market system was promoted as the prime mechanism for economic success. Lying somewhere in between are the developmental and corporatist models that reflect the economic mixture of 'private' and 'public' ownership. Institutions are created to cement state and industry in a common bond to produce policies that are directional and proactive. Each country devises its own collection of

1

institutional practices with differing emphasis in such areas as industrial regulation, organised labour and health.

All vocational education policy development is underpinned by a particular model of industrial policy and requires some degree of consensus between the participant policy makers. This book is about the formulation of vocational education policy where the main theme is the achievement of consensus – denoting a judgement that reflects the group solidarity of those involved. Who takes part in the process, their power and influence, is determined by that synthesis of ideology and action that defines the industrial policy of different political regimes. This is shown clearly in the chapters that describe how vocational education is organised within Finland and the United States.

The liberal democratic concern over who legitimately has a voice in the proceedings of policy development has given rise to the notion of the 'stakeholder' – defined for our purpose as an individual or group whose participation is critical to the long-term progressive development of an undertaking where diverse interests compete for advantage. Some argue that the consensus that emerges from such stakeholder policy developments is more likely to find a solution to the problem, apparent from Taiwan to the United States but less so in Finland, of undue preference for academic rather than vocational education. The stakeholder consensus thus may be more inclined to promote the equalisation of esteem that will realise the recognition, compliance, commitment and conformity of the individual learner in pursuit of long-term personal advantage.

These concerns led the Scottish School of Further Education (SSFE) in the University of Strathclyde and the Advisory Scottish Council for Education and Training Targets (ASCETT) to organise jointly a Glasgow seminar in February 1996, and it is our wish that contributions from around the world presented in this book assist those who have an interest or are actively engaged in the development of vocational education.

# 1

# STAKEHOLDERS, CONSENSUS, PARTICIPATION AND DEMOCRACY

*Ian Finlay*

In this book we attempt to identify how consensus on VET (vocational education and training) policy is sought in a number of countries where interesting models have emerged. The focus of the book is on the principles of stakeholding and consensus applied to policy formulation and implementation in vocational education and training. The international case studies provide sound examples of practical strategies which have been successfully implemented and will be of interest to policy-makers, practitioners and academics.

Why are some countries more successful than others at involving stakeholders, social partners or role players in the formulation and implementation of education and training policy? How do these countries achieve consensus among the stakeholders? To what extent is consensus desirable or achievable in pluralist societies? What factors need to be taken into account in the development of policy in education and training if consensus and participation are seen to be desirable? These are the questions that are addressed in this book through a series of international case studies on the process of change.

Many developed and developing nations are looking to their VET systems to provide a response to changes in the global economy. Our earlier research (Finlay and Niven 1996) indicated that some countries are proactive with respect to these changes, adopting long-term strategies that should benefit their economies. Of the countries covered in this book, Finland, Germany, Ireland, Singapore and Taiwan would fit into this proactive category. The strategies adopted by these countries include coordinating economic, industrial and VET policies. Some such countries have also developed strategies for achieving consensus among the major stakeholders in the VET system. For example, in Germany a high level of consensus towards economic, industrial and VET policy is achieved through meaningful involvement of all the social partners. These social partners include federal and state

3

government, both sides of industry, and educational interests. Relationships between the social partners are governed by both federal and state legislation. The German model is only one example of a consensus-seeking strategy. Other countries seem to succeed economically with limited consensual participation. In truth all systems attain some measure of consensus or they would be unable to operate; this book describes how consensus is achieved in a number of different countries.

The material for this book emerged from a seminar which was held in Glasgow in March 1996 and which was organised by the Advisory Scottish Council for Education and Training Targets and the University of Strathclyde. Expert witnesses from seven nations presented papers and then held discussions on the theme of consensus and stakeholding in policy making. The book is an edited collection of these topical papers, with an introductory chapter by one of the editors and the addition of a chapter on changes in VET in Scotland.

It is important at this stage to justify our selection of comparator nations. To some extent, the editors' selections for a book such as this will be influenced by their own network of contacts and their knowledge and experience of other educational systems. This was an influence in our selection: we wanted to use nations that demonstrated some of the characteristics we felt worthy of exploration and we also wanted to use authors in whom we had confidence. We also had other, more objective, criteria that we used in making our selection.

Some countries were selected because of their economic strength. The United States, Germany, Singapore and Taiwan are in this category. These four countries were also selected because their education and training systems have generated interest and have been reported upon in the United Kingdom (see, for example, Cantor 1989; Ainley 1990; HMI 1990, 1991; Felstead et al. 1994; Ashton and Sung 1994; OECD 1994). We have a particular national interest in Scotland, so we also selected countries that share common cultural, geographical and demographic characteristics with Scotland. Finland and Ireland were selected partly for this reason, but additionally because they appeared to offer models of the operation of stakeholder involvement and consensus-seeking in vocational education policy formulation and implementation that were worth exploring. South Africa offers a unique case study in political change because of its history. The change from the previous social structure to a democracy has amplified many of the tensions and paradoxes that normally surround political change. The South African government has recognised this and has set in place a number of systems and processes to deal with the changes. These systems and processes are of general interest.

The remainder of this chapter is divided into three sections. The first deals with the main issues that we are exploring in the book. These are the issues of stakeholding, consensus, participation and democracy in relation to the formulation and implementation of vocational education and training policy. It reviews the literature on these issues and sets out our stance. The next section summarises issues that were discussed at the expert seminar from which this book emerged. The final section summarises our current perspective.

## Stakeholding, consensus, participation and democracy

The relationships between major stakeholder groups involved in VET policy are illustrated in Figure 1.1. These groups can be described in a number of ways. In the United Kingdom during the 1960s and early 1970s these groups would have been referred to as social partners. Partnership was part of the prevailing discourse with membership of bodies such as the National Economic Development Council, the Manpower Services Commission and Industry Training Boards comprising representatives of both sides of industry, national and local government, and other key partners. Social partnership is still the prevailing discourse in European countries such as Germany and Sweden. In Germany all the groups outlined in Figure 1.1 are involved in the formulation and delivery of VET with federal government, state government, employers, (individually or through chambers of commerce or chambers of craft), education and individual learners each having clearly defined roles within the process. These roles are discussed by Willi Brand in Chapter 6.

In the middle of the 1970s, the social partnership discourse began to break down and was gradually replaced by the market discourse. In Britain the breaking point for education is often given as 1976 when the prime minister, James Callaghan, made his Ruskin College speech. In this speech Callaghan attacked the professional hegemony in education and suggested education should be more accountable to parents and employers. During the late 1970s and throughout the 1980s the language of business and the market gradually permeated education. Students, pupils and employers became referred to as clients or customers; educational institutions were referred to as providers; and key-words in the discourse of VET became accountability, quality, efficiency and effectiveness. Market-based reforms in VET were also instituted in other countries, most notably in New Zealand, which had a Labour government that in many ways introduced market reforms with greater enthusiasm than the Conservative governments in Britain and the United States.

The potential for a new discourse entered British policy when Tony Blair, then leader of the Opposition, made a speech in Singapore in which he announced his intention to create a stakeholder society in Britain. This concept widens out the market discourse. Traditionally markets are conceived of as being a means of communication and exchange between the suppliers of a product or service and those who may wish to purchase that

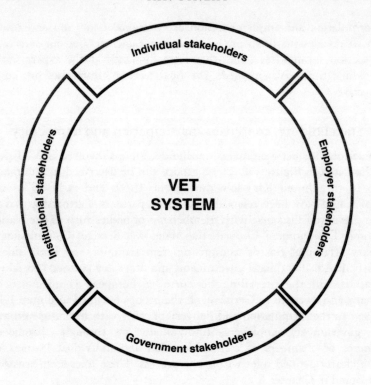

*Figure 1.1* The relationships between major VET stakeholders

product or service. Recent works on strategic management (e.g. Johnson and Scholes 1997) have suggested that companies need to look beyond their customers and shareholders when making decisions, and must take account of the effects of their actions on all groups or individuals who can influence, or who are affected by, the organisation's actions. These groups or individuals are known as stakeholders. Blair extended the use of the concept of stakeholder from the commercial to the political arena. This call to create a stakeholder society is potentially a move towards the creation of a participative democracy in VET policy formulation and implementation, but there are also critics who have pointed out that it is a further extension of the discourse of business into education (e.g. Gleeson 1996).

A final discourse draws on sociology rather than business, and is the terminology used in South Africa. This discourse uses the concept of role-players in the VET system. This discourse has some attraction in that having a role to play suggests active rather than passive involvement in the process of policy formulation and implementation. Other countries in our study use other terms: Rau writes in Chapter 4 of policy makers and general participants, and the chapter on Finland uses the term 'process owners'.

The groups illustrated in Figure 1.1 can be conceived of as social partners, as those with market-based relationships, as stakeholders, or as role-players, depending on the historical or national context being considered. In this chapter the term 'stakeholder' will be used to refer to those with an interest in VET policy. This term is also referred to by the authors of the other chapters, although they tend to use the terminology that is most frequently used in their own countries. The groups used in Figure 1.1 represent quite broad groupings and there is also likely to be some overlapping membership. Table 1.1 lists examples of individual stakeholders that could be included within each group.

There is no imputation in either Figure 1.1 or in Table 1.1 that power or influence is evenly distributed between either the four broad groupings of stakeholders or between individual stakeholders. At any time power or influence is likely to be unevenly distributed, and over time some stakeholders will increase in power or influence while others will see their position decline. In Britain the stakeholders that have suffered a long-term decline in influence have been professional educators, teaching unions (and unions in general) and local government, while employers and central government have seen major gains in power with respect to the VET system.

Our agenda is to promote the creation of participative, democratic processes in the formulation and implementation of VET policy. We see stakeholder involvement and consensus-seeking negotiation as being central to the creation of participative democracy. We agree that:

> the challenge now is to remake the values, purposes and institutional forms of the public domain so as to enable this democratic citizenship to be realised. Education is central to this remaking, for

*Table 1.1* Examples of stakeholders

| Individuals | Institutions | Government | Employers |
|---|---|---|---|
| Students | Universities | Central government | Multinationals |
| Pupils | Colleges | Local government | Small/medium enterprises |
| Trainees | Schools | Individual government departments | Public sector |
| Parents | Training organisations | Government-sponsored administering bodies | Private sector |
| Lecturers | Trade unions | Political parties | Employers' federations |
| Teachers | Examining bodies Professional bodies | | |

the task of realising cooperative action will require learning to be placed at the centre of our experience ...

(Ranson *et al*. 1997: 117)

Diani proposed both strong and weak definitions of participation. We would concur with his justification for a strong definition:

given the size and complexity of contemporary mass societies, the centralisation of political power, the growth of bureaucracy, and the concentration of economic power, the traditional guarantees of democracy need to be strengthened, protected and extended in order to counterbalance the tendency for an ever-increasing number of decisions affecting people's lives to be made by small groups; these groups are often remote and not easily identifiable or called to account, since they act in the name of the state, of a local authority, or of some large business organisation.

(Diani 1993: 448)

Over twenty years earlier Pateman had challenged the idea that achieving participative democracy is unrealistic in a large, complex, modern society. She also rejected the notion that the majority are apathetic to full participation arguing that what is taken as apathy may be a lack of socialisation into the participative process. She suggested that 'we do learn to participate by participating and that feelings of political efficacy are more likely to be developed in a participatory environment' (Pateman 1970: 105).

McNay and Ozga (1985) criticised the supporters of pluralism and consensus in the past for their failure to address questions about the function of education and of state power in education. Yet what we are arguing for is a deeper and wider consensus achieved through a process of negotiation and bargaining in which the participants explore the issues of values, power and assumptions, and make decisions to move forward in full recognition of these issues. We, with Giddens (1994), are arguing for the development of a 'dialogic democracy'. Singh puts it very well:

Because of the inherent conflict between different value perspectives which is to be found in cultural, pluralistic democracies and because of the dilemma inherent in autonomy based liberalism (which by its own tenet must allow different cultural and political groups to exist), the most we can achieve in a democracy is an untidy compromise between all groups. This paper assumes that such compromises stand a better chance of achieving social harmony and preserving individual dignity and respect if they evolve from discussions and negotiations.

(Singh 1997: 170)

Words such as stakeholder, consensus, participation and democracy are used symbolically in political discourse. Williams (1976) writes of 'key-words' which connect 'particular uses, similarities, dissimilarities and changes in the way they are understood'. Edelman (1977) writes that 'One aspect of symbolic political language is the condensation symbol, which evokes the emotions associated with the situation' (both quoted from Poulson 1996: 579). Stone provides a particularly cogent account of the symbolic use of words in politics. She writes:

> A symbol is anything that stands for something else. Its meaning depends on how people interpret it, use it, or respond to it. ... The meaning of a symbol is not intrinsic to it, but is invested by the people who use it. In that sense symbols are collectively created. Any good symbolic device, one that works to capture the imagination, also shapes our perceptions and suspends skepticism, at least temporarily. These effects are what make symbols political devices. They are means of influence and control, even though it is often hard to tell with symbols who is influencing whom.
>
> (Stone 1988: 108)

One powerful aspect of symbols is their ambiguity. Stone argues that ambiguity allows coalitions and helps to bring about cooperation and compromise. There is certainly ambiguity around words like stakeholding, participation, democracy and consensus. For example, Morris suggests that increasing the level of participation in the educational policy arena could be about things like 'decentralisation, power-sharing and political pluralism' (1996: 319) or it could be a means of continuing control by the current elite. Morris was reflecting on changes in Hong Kong. De Clercq also suggests that 'dialogue, negotiation and consensus' (1997: 134) can be used as means of maintaining the privilege, or at least not seriously undermining the privilege, of the existing elite. She argues that the White Paper on Education and Training in South Africa 'was a symbolic policy document ... designed to reassure all stakeholders with uncontroversial educational principles and values ... ' (1997: 134–5). In the United Kingdom, Gleeson states that stakeholder is a *spin-doctored* concept' (his italics) which 'may further camouflage such underlying patterns of social and economic inequality [as exist]' (1996: 519).

Changes brought about as a result of stakeholder involvement, through a participative democratic process are likely to be gradualist and evolutionary rather than revolutionary. Such changes are unlikely to immediately provide major challenges to the existing order since the existing order will be a major stakeholder constituency involved in the change process. This process ought to lead to change which is deeply rooted and which enjoys wide support.

It has been argued (e.g. Brittan 1975) that the market is the most effective mechanism for engaging the participation of the widest range of
citizens. Brittan titled his paper 'Participation without Politics'.
Participation without politics can also be participation without power if one
is relying on the market mechanism. Democracy is a means of ensuring that
all citizens have a voice in decision-making irrespective of income, wealth or
social position. It can thus be seen that markets are inherently undemocratic
since they distribute power on the basis of wealth or income. They are far
more effective than participative democracy at ensuring the continuing
hegemony of the elite. Markets, while being nominally neutral in their allocation mechanisms and universal in participation, are essentially
undemocratic if, by democracy, we mean giving voice independently of
wealth or class. Ranson *et al.* (1997) see the neo-liberalism of the 1980s and
1990s as a phase between the period of social democracy (up to the 1970s)
and the participatory democracy of the future. Our aim in this book is to
identify the degree to which other countries have been able to achieve a
participative democracy and to discover the practical mechanisms through
which they have done this in effecting change in vocational education and
training.

Figure 1.2 illustrates one simple model of change which includes
consensus-building in its framework. Change is at the centre of the model
and is surrounded by different kinds of political and research activity which
generate the knowledge to inform the change. Consensus-building takes
place in the interaction between the change and these activities.

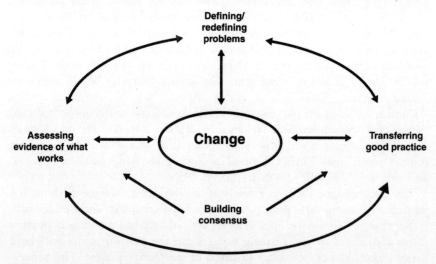

*Figure 1.2* Simple model of consensus-based change
*Source*: Joseph Rowntree Foundation

## Principles for achieving consensus

The authors agree that change is a long-term, complex and messy process. There are no easy blueprints for change. There is, however, also agreement on some principles and concepts which could guide the change process particularly with respect to achieving consensus. These are outlined below:

### *Recognition of the need for change*

Often a recognition of the need for change is a reaction to external stimuli. Fear, a traumatic event, a competitive threat, a set of precipitatory events, or a common enemy can lead to a groundswell for change. These stimuli are essentially reactive. The traumatic events in South Africa have led to a recognition of both a need for change and that the changes must be conducted in a manner which achieves the widest possible consensus. Bellis reports on the resulting process in Chapter 9. In the United States, a series of precipitatory events such as the publication of international statistics on education and training performance and a sense of poor economic performance when compared with Japan and the emerging economies of South East Asia, led to a recognition of the need for change. Betsy Brand provides her analysis of change in the United States in Chapter 8.

Change can also be recognised as an evolutionary process which is integrated into the education and training system. The way change is approached in Finland exemplifies this approach.

### *Consensus within a pluralist society*

Singh (1997) inferred that there is a possible tension between achieving consensus and retaining a pluralist society. This tension is also recognised by the authors of this book. Could the attempt to achieve consensus about policy change lead to some of the stakeholders having to concede some of their values? We think not.

Rawls (1993) writes of the idea of 'overlapping consensus', suggesting that it is possible to reach agreement on some things without being in agreement on everything. This approach is exemplified in the South African case-study. In a working group in which the members had a diverse range of interest- and value-positions, some directly opposed to others, agreement was reached on a set of shared values about education while group members retained very different political and religious values. The same approach has operated in Ireland. It is represented in Figure 1.3.

In achieving consensus it is possible to have all parties accept the outcomes without necessarily agreeing on everything, provided they are all able to 'live with' those outcomes. Respect for, and inclusion of, all the

11

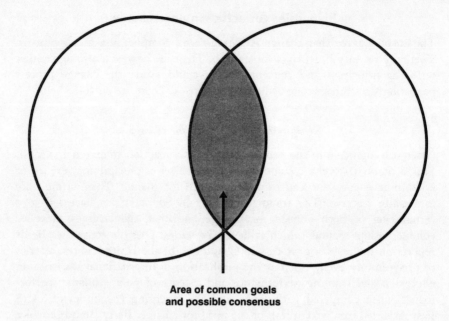

**Area of common goals
and possible consensus**

*Figure 1.3* Venn diagram illustrating consensus

appropriate stakeholders are seen to be important in achieving the acceptability of the outcomes.

### Consensus as a process

Consensus is seen by the authors as being a long-term, continuing and iterative process. It is seen as an attempt to move away from doing things to people or for people to doing things with people. It is also seen as an attempt to move away from hierarchies towards networks. Moving to networks is not without problems. Networks are not necessarily more democratic than hierarchies if they remain exclusive. The shift to networks must be accompanied by wider involvement if democracy is to be enhanced. The issue of who to involve is addressed in the next section.

Different skills are required to successfully work in a network from those required for successful operation in a hierarchy. Influencing rather than directing is important. Both formal and informal communications have a place in the process. It is felt that even if the outcomes can be predicted beforehand, it is still important to go through the process of seeking consensus since the process itself adds value.

## Identifying stakeholders

The stakeholders invited to take part in the policy formation and implementation process vary from country to country. There are key questions that ought to define stakeholder involvement:

Which stakeholders should be included?
How will they be identified?
How credible and representative are those who are invited to participate?
Who are the key stakeholders whose agreement must be sought?
Which vested interests will need to be involved?
How widely will the stakeholder net be cast?

Different stakeholders have different spheres of influence. In her chapter on the United States, Betsy Brand points out that the sphere of influence of parents is at the local level whereas policy makers have influence at federal, state and local levels. Even within stakeholder groups, interests are not homogeneous. This makes finding representative stakeholders particularly difficult.

## Leadership and consensus

Leadership rather than leaders is seen to be important. A leader has to emerge who can create the vision and then find others to lead groups of stakeholders. These leaders must be able to interpret for and communicate with their own groups. The consensus is achieved through a coalition of leaders.

A key leadership role, in achieving consensus, is fulfilled by facilitators. These are honest brokers who ideally do not have a stake in the outcomes but who are skilled in focusing groups on the key issues. Help can be provided by 'window people' who present the group with different views, and 'door people' who provide access to required resources.

## Values, vision and language

Some societies, for example those in eastern Asia, have a common set of traditional values encompassing religion, family, respect for business, education, work and respect for individuals. If these common values do not exist then the process of achieving consensus is different and probably more difficult. The importance of developing a shared vision, a common set of values and a common understanding of basic terms are three philosophical areas that have to be sorted out prior to a consideration of processes or structures.

The issue of reaching shared values was discussed in an earlier section which focused on achieving consensus within groups coming from widely disparate social, political and religious backgrounds. In achieving a common philosophical framework, respect for other views and inclusion of those with opposing views are seen to be important.

One way of achieving this common approach is to reach early agreement on the key goals. Some of these goals may be long-term ideals to be achieved. By focusing on goals rather than structures or processes in the early stage, value positions become clarified and areas of common concern rather than areas of difference come to the fore. Differences, however, must be recognised and not pushed under the carpet. The leadership and facilitators have a key role here.

The creation of vision and common values are closely related to each other and to a third area, that is achieving agreement on common meanings of key terms and basic assumptions. In this area issues such as agreement on the current situations and the interpretation of research findings, gaining consensus on concepts and meanings, and moving away from traditional towards more open thinking are important.

### Partners and processes

In attempting to achieve consensus in the policy-making process, a deep cut down through the strata of interested parties is required. There must be top-to-bottom and bottom-to-top involvement. This can be achieved in some innovative and non-traditional ways. For example, groups which have been previously excluded from the policy-making process can be given resources to conduct research in their areas of concern.

The process should start with the assumption that all the stakeholders will have an interest at some point in the process. Thus it is essential that the process is iterative and the same issues are addressed involving an ever-widening circle of stakeholders. The process can be illustrated as a gyre or upward, ever-widening spiral (see Figure 1.4).

In the process, all the partners need to model the behaviours that are being sought, for example risk-taking, caring, openness, fun, and being comfortable in expressing views. An early task of the group initiating the process, is to create a framework process designed to find solutions to perceived problems. Multilevel planning is seen to be one helpful framework which embodies the gyre principle.

Figure 1.5 illustrates the levels of activity at which planning and progress need to be made. Different approaches need to be developed to deal with planning at each of these levels. The external influences at the visionary/blue-sky level are likely to be social, political and economic trends which may be difficult to anticipate. At the strategic and operational levels, pressures will be coming in from the constituencies of the various stakeholders, but if the involvement of stakeholder groups is sufficiently comprehensive, then feedback to these constituencies should be available

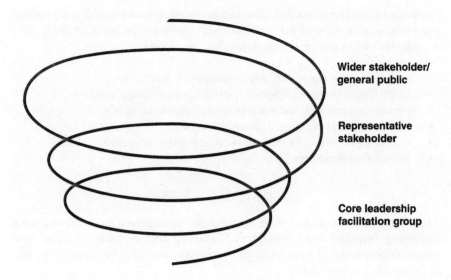

*Figure 1.4* The ever-widening spiral of stakeholders

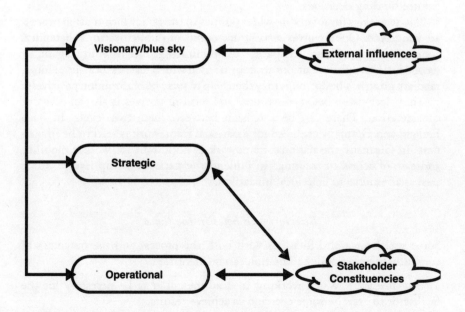

*Figure 1.5* Levels of activity for planning and progress

through their representatives. The success of the process will depend on the extent to which the agendas of the various constituencies are dealt with.

The following practical suggestions on the process, are offered:

- strategic mapping of partners at different levels
- identifying circles of influence – drivers, moderators, blockers
- conducting research and analysis with the general public
- identifying and tackling differences upfront
- having a procedure for dealing with new issues that arise
- conducting action research.

### Communication and politics

This section is concerned with getting the message across to others, with receiving feedback from others, with making the necessary changes, and most importantly with getting the proposals accepted by those with the power to implement them.

Communication needs to be two-way and iterative. Giving people a one-off chance to make a response to official documents does not constitute consultation. Gleeson's quote from Streeck and Schmitter (1985: 131) is apposite in this context 'ultimately the purpose of partnership ... involves much more than just a right to be consulted by the government on legislation. Essentially, it means sharing in the state's authority to make and enforce binding decisions.'

Two strategies for involving wider publics in the policy formulation process are suggested. One involves setting up rounds of public hearings: listening, communicating, taking feedback, communicating and listening again. A second is that a public relations strategy be used which reaches local-level intermediary groups. These groups may then help to sway public opinion positively.

The relationship between national and local initiatives is also an issue for consideration. There can be a tension between these two levels. In both Finland and Germany the need for a national framework is seen to be important. In Germany the national framework is important for worker mobility and ease of access to training. In Finland the national set-up is very much seen as a resource to help local initiatives.

### Barriers and holes in the fence

Some problems and difficulties with both the process and the outcomes of consensus-seeking policy formation can be identified:

*Time constraints.* When working to deadlines, it may be necessary for the facilitator to exercise some coercion to achieve results.

*Disagreements.*    There will be issues which cannot be agreed. Put these to one side and re-visit them later.

*Implementation.*    Implementation is always difficult. The policy formation process should be designed to make implementation easier.

*Hidden agendas.*    Some partners may have hidden agendas; this can be tackled by producing interim outcomes before reaching a final conclusion.

*Wrong solutions.*    Poor or wrong solutions can be reached through consensus. Evaluate solutions against initial goals to check their integrity.

*Flexibility.*    Initiators need to accept that they are not always right.

### What has worked elsewhere?

The following are examples of initiatives that have been successful in the process of involving wider groups than is traditional in the formulation of policy.

*High level, high visibility conference.*    A good example of this is the National Education Convention held in Dublin from 11 to 21 October 1993. This 'provided a forum for mature reflection and focused debate by representatives of many of the agencies involved. It set out to encourage participants to clarify viewpoints; to question, probe and analyse varying perspectives; to foster multi-lateral dialogue and improve mutual understanding between sectoral interests; to explore new ways of doing things; and to identify areas of actual or potential agreement between different interest groups' (Coolahan 1994: 1).

*Reports and research.*    Räty reports that the process of change in Finland 'had many experimental phases where the new initiatives were tested and accepted'. In Scotland the pilot research projects are not always given a long enough run, nor are they sufficiently evaluated prior to full implementation. Again the idea of funding community groups and other stakeholders previously excluded from the policy process to conduct research and development work has worked elsewhere. It is part of the strategy in South Africa, for example.

*Demonstration/innovative projects.*    The Tech Prep materials produced by the Center for Occupational Research and Development in Texas are a good example of an attempt to address a perceived need in an innovative way. The adoption of these materials in most American states (and in other countries) has been the result of a lengthy period of evangelising, negotiation and demonstration.

*International study tours.* These help to overcome two problems in policy formation. The first is the idea that there are no alternatives to the way we do things. But there are always alternatives, some of which may be more effective than our ways. To believe that there is no alternative stifles creativity and progress. The second potentially problematic idea is that the grass is always greener elsewhere. Some patches may well be greener than some of our patches, but others are also looking enviously at our field. International study tours help to develop an accurate perspective of both our own and other VET systems.

## Perspectives of change

Our own perspective on the change process has developed while we have been researching and writing this book. When we started we had a modernist and optimistic agenda. We attempted to discover a process or recipe for change using participative methods which would achieve consensus among the stakeholder groups. We are probably less optimistic and more post-modern in our current perspective. The messages from the case studies reported in the following chapters are that there are alternatives to the market mechanism to achieve participation but there are also many contradictions, paradoxes and inconsistencies in practical politics. The maintenance of existing privilege, the tendency by all governments to control, and the perception of lack of efficiency of full democratic participation, mean that we have no examples of participative processes at all levels in any single country. However, we are no less committed to the principles of participative democracy in the reform of vocational education and training. The international dialogue that has underpinned the research upon which this book is founded, must be carried on at national and local levels if such democracy is to be effective. Hopefully this book will contribute to, and inform, that dialogue.

## References

Ainley, P. (1990) *Vocational Education and Training*, London: Cassell.
Ashton, D.N. and Sung, J. (1994) *The State, Economic Development and Skill Formation: A New Asian Model*, Working Paper 3, Leicester: Centre for Labour Market Studies.
Brittan, S. (1975) *Participation without Politics*, London: Institute of Economic Affairs.
Cantor, L. (1989) *Vocational Education and Training in the Developed World: A Comparative Study*, London: Routledge.
Coolahan, J. (ed.) (1994) *Report of the National Education Convention*, Dublin: Government Publications.

de Clercq, F. (1997) 'Policy intervention and power shifts: an evaluation of South Africa's education restructuring policies', *Journal of Education Policy* 12 (3): 127–46.

Diani, M. (1993) 'Participation', in W. Outhwaite and T. Bottomore (eds) *The Blackwell Dictionary of Twentieth-century Social Thought*, Oxford: Blackwell.

Edelman, M. (1977) *Political Language: Words that Succeed and Policies that Fail*, New York: Academic Press.

Felstead, A., Ashton, D., Green, F. and Sung, J. (1994) *International Study of Vocational Education and Training in the Federal Republic of Germany, France, Japan, Singapore and the United States*, Leicester: The Centre for Labour Market Studies.

Finlay, I. and Niven, S. (1996) 'Characteristics of Effective Vocational Education and Training Policies: An International Comparative Perspective', *International Journal of Vocational Education and Training* 4 (1): 5–22.

Giddens, A. (1994) *Beyond Right and Left: The Future of Radical Politics*, Cambridge: Polity Press.

Gleeson, D. (1996) 'In the Public Interest: Post-compulsory Education in a Post-modern Age', *Journal of Education Policy* 11 (5): 513–26.

HMI (1990) *Aspects of Education in the USA: Vocational and Continuing Education*, London: HMSO.

—— (1991) *Aspects of Vocational Education and Training in the Federal Republic of Germany*, London: HMSO.

Johnson, G. and Scholes, K. (1997) *Exploring Corporate Strategy*, 4th edn, London: Prentice Hall.

McNay, I. and Ozga, J. (eds) (1985) *Policy Making in Education: The Breakdown of Consensus*, Oxford: Pergamon Press with the Open University.

Morris, P. (1996) 'The Management of Participation in the Policy Making Process: The Case of the Education Commission in Hong Kong', *Journal of Education Policy* 11 (3): 319–36.

OECD (1994) *Vocational Training in Germany: Modernisation and Responsiveness*, Paris: OECD.

Pateman, C. (1970) *Participation and Democracy*, Cambridge: Cambridge University Press.

Poulson, L. (1996) 'Accountability: A Key-word in the Discourse of Educational Reform', *Journal of Education Policy* 11 (5): 579–92.

Ranson, S., Martin, J. and Nixon, J. (1997) 'A Learning Democracy for Cooperative Action', *Oxford Review of Education* 23 (1): 117–31.

Räty, O. (1996) *Quality Practises {sic} in VET Reforms in Finland*, University of Strathclyde/ASCETT International Seminar, Hilton Hotel, Glasgow, 29 February–1 March 1996: 6.

Rawls, J. (1993) *Political Liberalism*, New York: Columbia University Press.

Singh, B.R. (1997) 'Liberalism, Communitarianism and Discussion Method', *Educational Studies* 23 (2): 169–84.

Stone, D.A. (1988) *Policy Paradox and Political Reason*, Glenview, IL: Scott Foresman.

Streeck, W. and Schmitter, P. (1985) 'Community, Market State and Associations? The Prospective Contribution of Interest Governance to Social Order', *European Sociological Review* 1 (2): 119–38

Williams, R. (1976) *Keywords*, London: Fontana.

# 2

# STAKEHOLDERS AND PARTNERS IN VOCATIONAL EDUCATION AND TRAINING IN SCOTLAND

*John Fairley*

## Introduction

The terms 'stakeholder' and 'partner' are much more complex than they appear at first sight. Both are difficult to define with precision. They may overlap in so far as a 'stakeholder' may also be a 'partner'. Each term may carry baggage of an ideological or political nature. Their precise meanings evolve over time, shaped by the society which employs them.

In vocational education and training (VET) both terms are found, though 'partnership' is more commonly employed in Scotland. In VET the use and definitions of the terms has changed over time, and continues to develop. The devolution of certain VET responsibilities to the Scottish Office means that aspects of 'partnership' which used to be defined at a UK/British level are being reformulated better to reflect the situation in Scotland.

While VET has become more 'Scottish' as a result primarily of the reforms of the 1990s (Fairley and Paterson 1991), and differs in many ways from VET elsewhere in the UK, the Scottish system is far from simple. It shares common elements with other parts of the UK and has features which are distinctive and unique. It contains a number of different types of institution, each of which is changing under different pressures. Within the overall complexity (Fairley 1996a) different types of partnership are to be found at different levels, and one institution may find itself in a range of partnership relations.

Following a discussion of the 'stakeholder' and 'partnership' concepts, this chapter will examine the evolution of stakeholding and partnership in different levels of the VET system. Industrial VET will be examined, as will VET which aims to combat unemployment. The unique institutions of Scottish VET in the 1990s will be discussed, as will the emerging Scottish decision-making frameworks of the European Union.

## Stakeholders and partners

The concept of 'stakeholder' is employed in discussion in Scotland, but perhaps it is more employed in discussions of management than of policy. Contemporary management thinking, particularly as it affects the public sector, promotes the virtues of 'being competitive' and of reducing management hierarchies and their associated costs. A key task of the new, slimmer management-structure is to identify the main 'stakeholders' in the particular public service, with a view to empowering key stakeholders individually or through inclusion in partnership arrangements. In the 1990s the public service 'customer' is generally viewed as the most important stakeholder.

In VET the main stakeholders would include the trainee, the actual or potential employer, the training provider, the training funder and the taxpayer. Trade unions would not generally be regarded as major stakeholders having lost influence throughout the 1980s (Fairley 1993), but some unions do influence some VET programmes through collective bargaining machinery. The term stakeholder may be applied to an individual or to a collective organisation.

In some areas of VET, as across a wide range of public policy, attempts have been made to identify and prioritise the 'stake' held by the individual 'customer' or the 'end-user' of services. In a few areas of VET – an example is the Skillseekers programme for 16–19 year olds – an attempt has been made to introduce what the popular management writers Osborne and Gaebler (1993) call 'customer driven budgets'. In Skillseekers a degree of 'stakeholder empowerment' or 'customer choice' is provided through the mechanism of vouchers with a monetary value which are used to purchase the individual's training.

The prioritisation of the customer by much of contemporary public policy as the most important stakeholder, provides one reason for a certain degree of caution over the use of the term in VET in Scotland. In this form the 'stakeholder' is an individual and the concept comes shaped by the market-place. Even though 'customer-focused' management changes have largely been welcomed in Scotland, the competitive and individualistic agenda of the market-place enjoys no such popularity, and has been actively opposed in education (Pignatelli 1994). Scotland sees itself as more corporatist than England (Brown *et al*. 1996) and confidently promotes its collectivist approach to education (EIS/SCC 1996). There is a certain degree of unease in Scotland over some aspects of the stakeholder debate.

A further reason for a certain reluctance to use the term comes from its recent politicisation. The main political party in Scotland, the Labour Party, has adopted the phrase 'stakeholder society' to describe its vision of a future Britain. The leader of the Labour Party in Scotland, George Robertson MP, has called for the creation of a 'stakeholder economy – an economy in which opportunity is available to all, advancement is through merit and from which no group or class is set apart or excluded' (Robertson 1996). Scotland generally regards itself as a 'consensual' society and there is a widespread reluctance to employ terminology which is perceived to be politicised. Nevertheless, despite these concerns increasingly 'stakeholders' are acknowledged. In some cases they and their rights are recognised and defined in law, though this is perhaps less true of VET than other areas of public policy.

The 'stakeholder' has 'an interest' in an area of policy or in a publicly-funded service. The stakeholder interest may be 'weak' or 'strong'. In the former case the interest may simply be noted by decision-makers. Where the stakeholder interest is acknowledged to be strong then attempts will be made to give that interest 'voice' in the decision-making process or a full partner's role.

The stakeholder's interest may take a wide range of forms. Currently the interest of the customer receives some priority, but there are many other stakeholder interests. Where the stakeholder interest is important, special efforts are made to specify and protect it. In VET much more attention is paid to trainees and their interests than was the case in the 1960s and 1970s. However stakeholders would not normally play a direct role in policy-making, though in certain areas they may have rights to be consulted and rights of redress.

At particular points in the development of VET stakeholders have struggled to achieve or have been accorded a strong partnership role in decision-making. In the 1980s, through a series of reforms, the government sought to put private sector employers in the driving seat in order to make VET more market-responsive. These changes were controversial, and to some extent contested. In the 1990s the voluntary sector lobbied successfully for full partnership status in the decision-making bodies for the European structural funds. It campaigned on the basis of its ground-breaking work in VET funded by the European Social Fund. Its widely supported campaign was successful.

'Partnership' is a stronger concept and is used much more in discussions of VET and education more generally in Scotland. Generally (though not always) a 'partner' is an organisation which speaks on behalf of a group of people. In VET the main partners may include employers' organisations, trade unions, colleges and training providers, the government and its agencies, and the European Union.

However 'partnership' too is difficult to define with precision and the term is often misused, not least in education. Raab (1993) notes that partnership may be an 'honorific term' and that it may be employed as part of a political game. An example here might be the claiming of 'partner status' for a stakeholder, perhaps to conceal relations of inequality or to exaggerate the importance of their role. School students and VET trainees are acknowledged as stakeholders in education who have rights, but they are rarely considered to be partners in policy-making. Humes (1994) suggests that the invocation of terms such as 'partnership' and 'consensus' in Scottish education may serve to conceal the highly centralised nature of the system. The VET reforms of the 1990s may provide some illustrations of this point.

The strength of public sector partnerships is cited as the main reason for the limited impact of market-inspired reforms on Scottish education (Pignatelli 1994). As we shall see this claim is less true in the case of VET, perhaps because in Scotland partnerships were largely reconstructed in the 1990s at the same time as market-inspired management reforms were introduced. Throughout the 1980s and 1990s the main institutions of VET introduced market forces and mechanisms into VET, raising some degree of suspicion and even opposition in what Harvie (1994) has called the 'collective consensus' of Scottish society.

Partnerships may be 'vertical' within a VET system, or 'horizontal' between parts of the system. They may be 'weak' or 'strong' in nature, for example advisory partnerships have a weaker position than those vested with executive powers. Partnerships may be voluntary and organic, or based in statute and state-sponsored. Partnership may be found in multi-partite decision-making *within* a VET organisation, or in joint-working and decision-making *between* VET and other organisations. The membership of partnerships frequently overlaps, which is perhaps one of the main reasons why they are held to be effective devices for creating and sustaining consensus.

Bastiani (1993) discusses weak and strong concepts of partnership in relation to the roles of parents in schooling. His composite definition may be relevant to VET. It emphasises: the sharing of power, responsibility and ownership; a degree of mutuality; shared aims and goals; and a commitment to joint action. Raab (1993) stresses that interaction is important alongside formal powers and responsibilities.

The benefits of partnership are usually considered to be: greater continuity in policy and programmes; the combination of public (and sometimes private) sector budgets; the improved decisions which may come from the joint deliberations of several perspectives; the institutional learning which comes from doing things together; and the linking of previously separate policy areas (for example, VET and business development). The problematic aspects of partnership are at present less discussed. They include the concealing of dominant ideologies; the masking of very unequal power relationships; the restricting of debate to issues with which partners felt comfortable; the exclusion of non-partners from key debates; and the confusing of roles and accountability. Increasing levels of public concern about governance issues may lead to more discussion of these issues. Where the negative aspects of partnership are not identified and challenged, the quality of governance may be impaired.

Partnership then is a stronger, more collective, more frequently employed and less controversial concept than stakeholder. However on the occasions when there has been controversy in VET in Scotland it has frequently been focused on the site where the two concepts come together. The issues of which stakeholders are prioritised or excluded, and which are accorded part-nership roles, have been controversial at points of change in the VET system, and to some extent remain unresolved issues.

## Industrial training

The main policies and institutional arrangements for industrial or sector-focused training have traditionally been made at the British level, with little Scottish distinctiveness (Fairley and Paterson 1991; Fairley 1995). However Scottish interests have been fully represented in corporatist decision-making structures and in partnership arrangements. In the 1980s and 1990s the government view of which partners should play a leading role changed sharply.

Up until the mid-1960s industrial training was regarded as a matter for employers to decide in the light of their trading and market position. Some of the state-owned public industries provided an exception in that aspects of their VET arrangements were defined in law. In industries where trade unions were strong, industrial VET was influenced through collective bargaining arrangements. These determined the size of the apprentice intake and apprentices' rates of pay, but did not usually take an interest in the educational aspects of VET, and often took no interest in non-apprenticed occupations. The education trade unions, principally the Educational Institute of Scotland, played a role in the management of the Further Education Colleges which were the main providers of off-the-job training.

In general the system was decentralised and voluntarist in nature. The partnerships which existed were voluntary and were formed at the level of the industrial sector. In industries where trade unions and employers' organ-isations were strong, they were the major partners in VET. But in general these arrangements were primarily formed for some other purpose, such as wage bargaining. VET in these situations was often an agenda item rather than the main focus of attention. And generally the thinking on VET was short-term.

By the early 1960s there was a strong consensus across the political parties and between the main employers' organisations and the trade unions that the voluntarist system was not working well. Skill shortages were perceived to be hindering economic expansion. Employers were agreed to be under-investing in skill formation, preferring instead to 'poach' skilled labour from their competitors, even if this meant a certain bidding up of the price of labour.

The 1964 Industrial Training Act brought an end to voluntarism and introduced new partnership decision-making bodies. The Act led to the setting up of twenty-seven Industrial Training Boards (ITB) which were independent of government. The 'scope' of these boards was based on the statutory definition of sectors of industry. The Act was clearly intended to cover the whole economy but a decision of the House of Lords limited the spread of the ITB system.

The ITBs were charged with raising the level of VET, equalising the funding of VET between firms in an industry by means of a powerful levy–grant mechanism, and collecting data on employment and training for planning purposes. The levy–grant power was the main instrument available to the ITBs and it was used to make progress on all of the objectives. The levies varied between industries according to the real costs of an adequate level of VET. Generally levies were imposed on the firm's wages bill, but four industries opted for a per capita levy. The highest levy was set at 2.5 per cent of payroll costs by the Engineering ITB (Perry 1976). Most ITBs had some means of exempting small firms as a matter of policy, or on simple cost benefit grounds. As the system developed, levies became more sophisticated. The Engineering and Chemicals and Allied Products ITBs varied their levies according to the size of firm. Part-time workers were exempted in agriculture.

The levies generated income which the ITBs used to fund grants schemes for their industries. These were intended to redistribute the costs of industrial VET by rewarding the good trainers and penalising those firms which had a poor record. There were three main types of ITB grant: the reimbursement of costs, the payment of fixed amounts, and the payment of grants as a proportion of levy.

ITB decisions were made in partnership. The key partners were defined as the employers and the trade union 'sides' of industry, and they were given equal numbers on the ITB boards. In the ITB system the key partners were the two sides of industry, and the levy–grant mechanism greatly increased the attention and priority accorded to VET at company-level and industry-level discussions.

Board members were government appointees and generally the term of appointment was for three years. Only the two main partners were able to vote which seemed to some stakeholders to confirm the continuing status of VET as an industrial relations issue. The Chairman of the Board was independent. The others present at board level were there to provide expertise in an advisory capacity. ITBs had advisers from the education sector and assessors from government departments on their boards. A larger ITB would have had nine trade union members, nine from the employers, and six others in advisory roles.

These arrangements considerably strengthened the roles played by trade unions in determining VET policy and practice at national level. The ITB machinery was designed to be consensual. Progress and change required the consent of both the main partners. And employers and trade unions were felt to constitute the decision-making community as far as industrial VET was concerned. The strength of this narrowly-based partnership was demon-strated in the early 1970s when joint pressure by the Confederation of British Industry (CBI) and the Trades Union Congress (TUC) persuaded the government to drop its plans to abolish the ITBs (Perry 1976).

The ITBs' operations had to deal with the distinctive characteristics of the Scottish education system, such as the school leaving certificate, school leaving dates and the structure of further education. However, only a few of the larger ITBs treated Scotland as a distinctive area of operation (Fairley 1982) and gave the country its own partnership arrangements.

The ITBs were loosely coordinated by the advisory Central Training Council (CTC). The CTC was broad and 'multi-partite' in its composition, giving roles to a wider range of stakeholders. While the CTC was supported by the employers and the unions, nevertheless it was a weak organisation. The trade unions in particular wanted it to be replaced by a stronger co-ordinating mechanism.

The Employment and Training Act of 1973 weakened the ITBs, and strengthened the central coordinating and planning mechanism. As far as the ITBs were concerned the replacement of levy–grant by the new device of levy–grant exemption weakened the main instrument at their disposal. As the economy faltered following the 1974 'oil shock', and as industry shed workers throughout the late 1970s, the training activity of industry declined and the ITBs could do little to stop this. The ITBs and their partic-ular form of VET partnership became less and less effective. And as far as the stakeholders who were outside of the narrow ITB partnerships were concerned (for example, educationalists and the voluntary sector) the emerging, decentralised partnerships around VET for the unemployed seemed to be more inclusive and to offer greater opportunities to influence decision-making.

The Act led to the funding of ITB operating costs directly by the state. Prior to this the operating costs had been met by the ITBs themselves from levy income. The change to state funding weakened industry's sense of 'ownership' of the boards, and seems to have influenced some employers who came to see the ITBs as part of government rather than as industry-based partnerships.

The Central Training Council was wound up and replaced by a powerful Manpower Services Commission. The new MSC retained the multi-partite character of its predecessor, giving the broad range of stakeholders a place in the strategic planning of VET. Wright (1989) described the MSC as a 'co-ordinating partnership'.

The MSC's main tasks were to coordinate the ITBs and handle the strategic planning of VET. However these were quickly overshadowed by its use as the main instrument for responding to the rapidly-growing problem of unemployment. The MSC's distinctive approach to partnership and the building of consensus are discussed below in that context.

Legislation of 1981 established a process by which training arrangements could be changed in favour of a return to voluntarism, reflecting the Conservative government's faith in market mechanisms. The Act allowed employers to devise voluntary VET arrangements and present these to the Employment Secretary. If they met published criteria the ITB could be wound up and replaced by the new voluntary arrangements. Major employers in important sectors like engineering had been lobbying government to introduce this type of change for some time (Senker 1992).

These new powers were used to establish, for a brief period in the 1980s, a new statutory ITB for the offshore petroleum industry. This was based at Montrose on the east coast of Scotland. By the mid-1990s all but two of the ITBs, including Offshore Petroleum, had been replaced by voluntary Industry Training Organisations. Only in Construction and Mechanical Engineering Construction, where employers could not bring forward acceptable voluntary proposals, were statutory ITBs retained.

The 1988 Employment Act finally changed the balance between the partners in the remaining ITBs, giving the major role to private sector employers. The old equal balance on the boards had shown itself to be good at building consensus but slow and weak at dealing with change. It was felt that the pace of industrial change required VET bodies which were more responsive to the market and which could keep pace with change. However, as important was the hostility of the new Conservative government to trade unions and its desire to weaken their influence.

By the mid-1990s there were well over 100 ITOs and most were very small organisations (Fairley 1995), although a few were based on former ITB structures. These were regulated by the Department for Education and Employment, and they constituted the only significant part of the VET system which had not been devolved to the Scottish Office by the mid-1990s.

Only of a handful of the ITOs were 'Scottish' in origin or in the location of their headquarters, though many operated in Scotland. In most cases the ITOs solely reflected the employers' interests, though a few of the larger ones retained links with trade union and education interests. In a sense the move to ITOs represented the end of the state-sponsored partnership principle as it had applied in industrial VET. This is not to say that other stakeholders ceased to have influence. Rather it is to say that the government saw its role as sponsoring only one set of stakeholders, the employers. The ITOs were perhaps an attempt to decentralise in order to promote ownership on the part of one set of partners (the employers) and through them to promote greater market-responsiveness for VET. The change was also an attempt to reduce the role of the state in industrial VET, and to reduce the influence of other partners, the trade unions in particular.

However, the fact that most ITOs were small required them to adopt a partnership approach to policy and to projects. And through partnership-working, other stakeholders were able to exert influence. Crucial to VET was the quality of the partnerships developed by the ITOs and the new, uniquely Scottish local bodies which delivered government-funded VET (Fairley 1995). The government argued that voluntary partnerships were more effective than statutory, representative bodies. The move to the ITOs also to an extent returned industrial VET to the realm of industrial relations. Since the announcement of government support for the Modern Apprenticeship programme in 1993–4, the trade unions have played a role in developing apprenticeship training frameworks in those industries where they exercise influence, for example, steel-making, knitwear, printing, road haulage, engineering and banking (TUC 1995).

## The Manpower Services Commission and the response to unemployment

The MSC's history and main programmes have been much discussed (Ainley and Corney 1990; Benn and Fairley 1986; Brown and Fairley 1989; Evans 1992; Finn 1987; Gleeson 1989). However, less attention has been paid to its distinctive contribution to partnership and the building of consensus in VET.

The MSC enjoyed the support of the main social partners from the beginning. The TUC in particular had long campaigned for the creation of such a body and identified very closely with the MSC (Jackson 1986). When the first Commission was constituted in February 1974 it comprised a full-time chairman and director, and nine part-time commissioners representing employers, trade unions, local government and education. As the MSC's role was increasingly dominated by its unemployment-focused VET programmes, membership was enlarged to include representatives of the voluntary sector. The voluntary sector and the local authorities provided a large proportion of the places on MSC programmes, particularly for the adult unemployed and particularly in Scotland (Maxwell 1989). The MSC structure allowed the two sectors to be decision-making partners as well as stakeholders. And the MSC's roles as strategist and as funder of training for the unemployed meant that the partners discussed a very wide range of issues.

In the late 1970s, in anticipation of Scottish devolution, the administrative responsibility for MSC programmes in Scotland passed to the Scottish Office, and a multi-partite Manpower Services Committee for Scotland was set up. The membership of the Committee mirrored that of the central Commission.

The MSC was highly centralised in its policy-making and programme design, a fact for which it was increasingly criticised during the 1980s. Employers, the voluntary sector and local authorities increasingly argued that VET and unemployment programmes must be tailored to the specificities of local labour markets, and that uniform national schemes were not effective. While it was highly centralised in its strategic functions, the MSC controlled a very decentralised delivery system, a regional advisory structure and a sophisticated machinery for wide-ranging consultations. These networks allowed a very wide range of actors to feel some involvement in and even 'ownership' of the MSC and its programmes. They also presented something of a paradox. While the old industrial partnerships were being weakened in order to empower employers, the MSC was developing an unprecedented range of opportunities for partnership involvement in VET and an inclusive style of management which appeared to contrast sharply with the rather narrow and increasingly ineffective practice of the ITBs.

The delivery system was designed really as a by-product of the official government view of the late 1970s that unemployment was only a short-term problem which would be solved by the next economic boom, and that therefore only . short-term unemployment palliatives were needed in response. The MSC quickly established a network of training providers who were paid and managed through contractual arrangements. In the late 1980s some 5,000 'managing agents' delivered the MSC's main programmes under contract (Committee of Public Accounts 1990). The view was that the supply of VET could be more quickly adjusted through this type of delivery system.

In many ways the MSC pioneered the 'quasi-market' approach to the delivery of public services. It organised the supply of VET on a contractual basis. It encouraged competition between suppliers to drive down costs and promote efficiency. In the much more cost conscious environment of the late 1980s a virtue was fashioned out of this expediency. Government applied practices which the MSC had pioneered throughout the public sector, including other areas of education. As the MSC sought efficiency savings from providers in the 1980s, many of these came to feel that they were junior stakeholders in VET rather then the MSC's genuine partners.

The MSC presided over a network of regional organisations which had advisory and administrative roles. Some of these were inherited but by the early 1980s the network had been tailored to meet the MSC's needs. In 1975–6 there was a network of 125 District Manpower Committees (DMC) throughout Britain. The DMCs and the smaller network of Special Programme Area Boards (SPAB) provided local forums in which the social partners could discuss the wide range of VET issues. In turn they helped to raise the level of local knowledge about VET.

In 1983, as part of its New Training Initiative, the MSC largely abolished the distinctions between its VET programmes for people in employment and its anti-unemployment schemes. The DMCs and the SPABs were replaced by fifty-five Area Manpower Boards (AMB), nine of which were in Scotland.

When the AMBs were set up, parliament was told that they would become local VET planning agencies with their own powers covering 'the whole spectrum of local training needs and provision' (Brown and Fairley 1989). This did not happen and the AMBs remained largely advisory, with a monitoring role in relation to the larger MSC schemes. On the occasions when an AMB publicly criticised or disagreed with the MSC, it was very quickly brought back into line. If the AMBs functioned internally as partnerships, their relationship with the MSC left virtually all of the power at the centre.

This power relationship was clearly illustrated in a dispute which was highly publicised at the time. The Central and Fife AMB disagreed with the MSC over operational issues. In the ensuing conflict the AMB's view was dismissed and it was overruled. The AMB chairman was John Pollock, the leader of the main educational trade union, the Educational Institute of Scotland. He publicly questioned the value and integrity of the AMB system.

The AMBs helped to mobilise and maintain consensus amongst the social partners at local level. This was crucial to the MSC and probably helped to contain trade union criticism as the unemployment schemes became more controversial during the 1980s. There is little doubt that the AMB system helped to legitimise approaches to VET and schemes which otherwise would have been the focus of public discussion. For over a decade, whenever a trade unionist or another AMB partner raised a doubt about MSC practices, the conclusion was invariably that it was best to stay with the AMB system and try to exert influence from within. The AMBs undoubtedly helped to raise awareness of VET issues at local level amongst a wide range of partners. Discussions took place in AMBs on the level of resources required to meet VET needs, applications for training schemes were assessed, and training provision was monitored. In the more active AMBs it seems likely that these discussions helped to raise the level of understanding of the nature of the unemployment problem and how the different partners viewed that problem.

The MSC also established a particular style of consultation which became more widely used during the late 1980s and 1990s. The MSC consulted widely amongst partners and stakeholders on any significant policy change and on its strategy updates. It consulted on strategic issues and at a rather general level. The consultations were generally successful at generating very broad support for the initiatives which the MSC wanted to take before they were introduced. At the same time, because consultations were at a rather general level, the MSC was left with a fairly free hand to work out the details of its approach. MSC consultations took the engineering of consensus to new levels, although there were frequent disagreements over points of detail once initiatives were introduced. One consequence was that debates and disagreements over VET between the partners tended to focus on points of detail – the level of trainee allowances, for example – rather than the broader strategic and policy issues.

Even with its many rather inclusive levels of partnerships, its decentralised system of delivering VET, and its particular consultative style, not every MSC initiative attracted consensus support. Two examples from Scotland illustrate this.

Scotland generally received 'its share' of MSC resources for centrally designed programmes, and although they were tailored to fit the country's education system, these were generally implemented in very much the same way as in the rest of Britain. However there was little enthusiasm among the major educational partners in Scotland – the Scottish Office, the Educational Institute of Scotland, and the local authorities – for the broader 'vocationalist' agenda of the MSC. In part this was because of the traditionally greater respect for vocational education in Scotland (Fairley and Paterson 1991) and the feeling that the new policy direction was unnecessary; in part it was due to the strong desire to maintain the historic autonomy of Scotland in education policy and so resist policies which were 'not invented here'; and in part it was due to the very strong commitment to the comprehensive principle, and the fear that the MSC's approach to vocationalism would undermine it (Paterson 1994).

The result of this complex process within which Scotland deployed its share of resources for common VET programmes but also tried to resist the MSC's homogenising vocationalism was to give a considerable boost to efforts to develop a distinctively Scottish approach to vocational education. By the end of the 1980s this was well in place, the first steps having been taken in the 1970s. And in Scotland the mainstream education system headed by the Scottish Office led the process. By contrast, in England MSC vocationalism was very much imposed on an often hostile education system.

The second example concerns the partnership difficulties which finally hastened the demise of the MSC at the end of the 1980s. Throughout the 1980s the trade union role in public policy generally was weakened by the government. But the British TUC remained a partner in the MSC and was intensely loyal to it. This policy stance affected trade unions in Scotland as well as their umbrella body, the Scottish Trades Union Congress (STUC), which tended to be more critical of the MSC.

During the 1980s, as the MSC sought efficiency savings from its training providers, it appeared to many trade unionists that the quality of government schemes declined, and that more pressure was put on unemployed people to accept training places. Two schemes in the late 1980s brought these feelings to the boil, the New Job Training Scheme (NJTS), and its successor, Employment Training (ET). These schemes seemed to many trade unionists to represent an end to voluntary participation and the beginnings of a compulsory 'workfare' type of programme. The STUC voted at its 1987 annual congress in Perth not to participate in the NJTS (Speirs 1989), the first time that the broad partnership sustaining the MSC had been broken in fifteen years. When the British TUC followed suit the following year

(Brown *et al*. 1996), the historic VET consensus engineered by the MSC was finally broken. The government moved quickly, first to exclude the trade unions from VET partnerships and so reduce their status and influence as stakeholders, and second to wind up the MSC itself.

## The new Scottish VET partnerships

In 1990, legislation paved the way for the emergence of distinctively Scottish VET institutions. The roles of the MSC and Scotland's two economic development agencies were brought together and given to two new non-departmental public bodies, Scottish Enterprise (SE) and Highlands and Islands Enterprise (HIE). The two new bodies were required by the Scottish Office to decentralise most of their work, including the provision of government-funded VET, to twenty-two Local Enterprise Companies (LEC) (Fairley and Lloyd 1995).

The LECs were to some extent modelled on the Private Industry Councils (PICs) in the United States, but they had more extensive powers than the PICs and the similar-sounding Training and Enterprise Councils (TECs) which were set up in England and Wales. Prior to the passing of the legislation the Scottish Office invited the private sector to form local consortia, draw up business plans, and bid for the work which the LECs would undertake for SE and HIE. The successful consortia went on to form the LECs in 1991.

The LECs were intended to bring VET and economic development closer together, to provide a local focus for policies and programmes, to provide VET and business support which was more relevant to small firms, and to involve the local private sector. The reform was also intended to give Scotland a distinctive VET system and it was followed by substantial devolution of responsibility for VET policy to the Scottish Office. This aspect of the reform addressed the widely-expressed view that the former MSC had been over-centralised and that some of its programmes had failed to recognise Scotland's VET needs.

The most controversial aspect of the change concerned the way in which the new bodies were to involve the private sector. The LECs were set up as companies operating under company law and were required to have two-thirds of their management boards drawn from the local private sector. This meant that the new publicly-funded bodies would have a private sector majority and a business *way of working*. The representative approach to partnership-working exemplified by the MSC was replaced by executive, unitary agencies. Individuals were invited on to the boards on their merit, to function as company directors and not to represent their sector. There was no right to representation for local authorities, the education sector, the voluntary sector or the trade unions. Once again partnership was redefined to prioritise the interests of the employers. On the industrial side this had been done by replacing the increasingly ineffective and narrow ITB partnerships.

As far as the unemployment programmes were concerned the multi-partite AMBs and the MSC's inclusive style were swept away and replaced by the LECs.

However the extent to which the LECs actually empowered local employers was quickly called into question. Certainly local employers had voluntarily come forward to form the bidding consortia from which the LECs emerged. But these arrangements only empowered the employers who had volunteered to get involved at the beginning of the process. Others felt left out. Once operational the LEC Board filled its own vacancies as members retired, leading to some criticisms (Scottish Affairs Committee 1995) that the LECs were not partnerships at all. Rather they were publicly-funded, self-perpetuating cliques. A survey carried out for the Federation of Small Businesses (FSB 1996) claimed that small firms were neither represented on nor well served by the LECs.

The former partners of the MSC felt very much left out. The government answered trade union critics by arguing that the unions had excluded themselves through their non-cooperation policy. But this argument did not address the position of other partners such as the voluntary sector, the local authorities and education who seemed also to be left out. Nor did it acknowledge the criticism that by narrowing the decision-making process, the government was simply excluding the expertise which had been accumulated by the social partners in the AMBs.

The LECs then represented a narrowing of the VET partnership and a fundamental change to the nature of decision-making processes. Once again the main reasons seem to have been a desire to empower local employers and through this to make VET more market-responsive. However it may also be the case that the characteristics of most of the LECs, the limitations on their budgets, and the nature of the environment in which they operated, encouraged or made necessary more partnership-working between institutions at local level than had previously existed.

The LECs ensure the delivery of VET by means of contracts with suppliers. Amongst these, the forty-three further education colleges are very important, but there is an estimated network of 800 suppliers. The regulation of the 'training market' by contracts and the continuing quest for efficiency savings mean that most of these suppliers see their LEC as purchaser and controller rather than partner. The larger colleges which are experienced and powerful in negotiations may be the exceptions.

Over the first few years LEC autonomy in VET increased but remained rather marginal in relation to their budgets. The House of Commons Scottish Affairs Committee (1995) was told that 95 per cent of LEC budgets remained tied to the central programmes of the former MSC. The need to continue delivering these schemes guaranteed some continuity in operational relationships to deliver VET. The LEC innovation may have changed the style of decision-making more than the patterns of working in the early years.

Certainly the limitations on autonomy in VET led to claims that the LECs simply served to mask the degree of central control. Against this claim it was argued that the LECs were relatively young organisations and that greater autonomy would be earned and granted as they matured. Some of the LECs critics, notably the Labour Party (Robertson 1996) and the STUC (1996) argued that too much was decentralised to the LECs in any case and wanted to see their limited autonomy reduced in order to strengthen the 'strategic core' of SE and HIE. However in their first five years the LECs did achieve some autonomy in VET. They managed to offer some locally-tailored VET programmes funded out of surpluses accumulated by delivering national schemes below budgeted costs, and by funding VET from their business development budgets. In these ways the narrow local partnerships demonstrated that they could add something of value to VET.

A few of the LECs – Glasgow, Lanarkshire, Edinburgh and Renfrew are examples – are large organisations. The majority are not. In the HIE network they are sufficiently small to justify the central provision of a number of support services. As relatively small and young organisations, the LECs have limited budgets and small staff teams. In many areas, including aspects of VET, small LECs lack in-house expertise. And the LECs are held accountable in part against comparative performance data. They are required to show good 'performance results' in the short term. All of these factors push the LECs towards partnership-working with other bodies. While this pressure offers some opportunities to partners who were constitutionally excluded from the LEC Boards, it is most likely to benefit those organisations with their own public sector budgets. The local authorities may benefit more than, for example, the trade unions or the voluntary sector.

The narrowing of partnerships through the LECs has brought new levels of criticism and controversy to VET in Scotland. Perhaps for the first time VET partnerships have been politicised. In early 1997, with a General Election looming, the four political parties had very different ideas about the future for the LECs. The Conservative government's quinquennial review (Scottish Office 1996) of SE, HIE and the LECs favoured retaining the system. The Labour Party (Robertson 1996) proposed broadening the LECs to make them representative of their communities, and ending their company status to make them local subsidiaries of SE and HIE. The Scottish National Party (SNP 1992 and 1996) proposed abolishing the LECs and making local development issues the preserve of elected local authorities. The Liberal Democrat Party (1996) proposed making the LECs accountable to new regional joint committees made up of representatives of local government and the further education sector.

## Colleges and local authorities

The environment in which the LECs operate has also changed in a number of ways since the 1990 Act. In 1992, forty-three further education colleges were removed from local authority control, given some degree of operational autonomy, and placed in a direct funding relationship with the Scottish Office. Separate funding relationships were put in place for three colleges in Skye and in the islands of Orkney and Shetland. The Act allowed for further establishments to be designated as further education providers.

The forty-three colleges were set up as incorporated bodies rather than companies, perhaps in an experiment with different forms of organisational autonomy. Once again employers were privileged with the main partnership role on college boards of management. And once again the main argument for this change was that employers would make VET more market-responsive and ensure that colleges were more efficiently run. Again one effect of the change was to narrow the partnership base. Leech (1994: 125) argued that a key effect of the change

> was to remove arguably one of the most significant groups of members from the further education system in Scotland, namely the local authorities. In particular the long-standing knowledge and experience gained by individual officers and advisers in managing further education policy, and the support and commitment of local authority elected members was formally severed.

The colleges have to some extent been freed to develop new initiatives and to compete with each other. This is producing some interesting VET initiatives, for example Lauder College's Gateway to Employment programme through which the college offers VET in partnership with other agencies in a variety of locations throughout Scotland. However, the colleges had a good record of innovation in their relationships with the MSC (Burness 1989), and it would be impossible to say whether the new set-up made colleges more or less innovative.

The new set-up for the colleges may have made them more inclined to be proactive and less inclined simply to respond to centralised VET programmes. Many of the colleges are large organisations with considerable VET expertise, and they may have come to feel that their links with the LECs are on a more equal footing than previous relationships with the MSC. Outside the main urban centres many colleges are in a near-monopoly supply position which is likely to give them considerable standing in their negotiations with the LECs over VET contracts.

The incorporation of the colleges weakened the local authority role in VET and removed some local authority expertise from VET. But local authorities retain responsibilities in adult and community education which overlap with VET, and control the school system. The development of the modularised National Certificate, and the Higher Still reforms which aim to give parity to vocational education within the school leaving certificate, will ensure that local authorities retain a strong role in VET. And since college incorporation there has been little evidence of any growth in competition between the school and college sectors. Research suggests that both wish to maintain the traditional, partnership, 'end-on' relationship (Finlay 1996).

In 1996, new all-purpose local authorities were set up throughout Scotland. LEC boundaries were altered in two areas to ensure coterminosity with the thirty-two councils. The councils were given a strong local influence in economic development for the first time (Fairley 1996b) and this together with their education role and their interests in tourism ensures a strong interest in VET. Generally the local authorities are large organisations compared with the LECs. Where previously councils may have felt the junior partners in relation to the MSC and the centralised development agencies, more equal partnerships with the LECs seem likely to develop.

## Qualifications and targets

In VET the qualifications framework is provided by the Scottish Vocational Education Council (SCOTVEC). One organisation, the Scottish Examinations Board (SEB) oversees school qualifications within which vocational elements, primarily SCOTVEC 'modules', became increasingly important in the late 1980s and 1990s. SCOTVEC and SEB were merged into a new, unified Scottish Qualifications Authority (SQA) in 1997, amid much discussion as to whether the ethos of the larger 'vocational' SCOTVEC or the older 'academic' SEB would prevail in the process.

Interestingly, both SCOTVEC and the SEB were established as partnerships broadly representative of the interest groups in their areas. Both became very powerful institutional stakeholders in Scottish educational debates and policy-making. While both existed, some differences of view between them emerged from time to time. The new SQA is also a representative partnership body. It looks likely to play an even more powerful role, in that it combines the previous roles, and brings to an end (or internalises) any competition between them.

The emerging VET system of the 1990s was decentralised and within its operations steps were taken to encourage and support the voluntary involvement of private sector firms. In order to provide some coherence to this system, and a degree of motivation to improve the system's performance, the Government established education and training targets. The targets set for Scotland were a little higher than for the rest of Britain in recognition of the generally better performance of the school system. A new partnership body, the Advisory Scottish Council for Education and Training Targets (ASCETT 1996) was set up to give leadership to this process, to research VET practice in other countries, to advise government on the targets which should be adopted, and to monitor and report on progress. The ASCETT Council is representative in nature. Half of the first ten-member Council was drawn from the private sector. The others came from local government, further education, the STUC, SCOTVEC and the SEB.

By 1997 ASCETT was already emerging as a powerful and influential stakeholder in the system. Its power derived from its influential members, from its unique relationship with government, and from the strongly consultative approach which it adopted. In 1994–5 the consultations involved some 9,000 people and 80 organisations (ASCETT 1996), providing a broad basis of support for its recommendations to government and helping to create consensus.

## The devolving partnerships of the European Union

The European Union (EU) has instruments of regional and social policy, the most important of which are known as the 'structural funds' (Danson et al. 1996). Some 85 per cent of Scotland's population lives in areas eligible for EU support through these programmes. When the smaller initiatives, some of which concern education and VET, are considered, the whole of Scotland is able to attract some EU funding.

The European Social Fund (ESF) is the main instrument as far as VET is concerned. In Scotland this operates as one national programme, the running of which has been largely decentralised from the Scottish Office to an external ESF Unit, based in Stirling. Within the partnership which oversees the ESF, the colleges form perhaps the most important and best organised sector. All forty-six are eligible for ESF support. Their organisation by the ESF Unit made them an influential partnership in accessing this funding source, and the strongest non-government 'sector' in the programme area.

The other structural funds are decentralised to seven area-based partnership bodies. This is distinctive within the UK and unusual within the EU. While the partnerships mostly focus on development issues rather than VET, all are concerned with VET to some extent (in the Objective 1 area of the Highlands and Islands, and the two Objective 2 areas, VET is very important). These partnerships are multi-partite (Danson et al. 1996) and consensual in their decision-making, although there is no clear role for trade unions and the private sector. The partners feel that relationships are based on equality and that decision-making has been improved by the breadth of perspectives involved.

Within the partnerships, three partners play particularly important roles. The Scottish Office chairs all seven groups and through this provides some degree of common approach to decision-making. The local authorities and the LECs are important because they have the budgets from which funding may be found to 'match' the EU contribution. The local authority involvement is through specialist officials. Scottish Office rules preclude the involvement of local elected politicians, which is quite different from the decentralised EU partnerships which are being developed in Sweden. And all partners work within the regulations and accountability framework devised by the EU.

## Conclusions

VET partnerships have changed considerably since the 1960s. From the 1980s government reforms have done away with the principle that partnerships should be broad and representative. Employers have been given privileged positions in decentralised sectoral and local VET bodies and in college management. The aims here have been to make VET provision more market-responsive, and to weaken the roles of other partners, notably the trade unions and the local authorities. However, the small size of many employer-led bodies has pressured them into more partnership-working with other VET agencies, and some of these local partnerships may be more equal than previous central-local VET relationships.

In the programmes sponsored by the EU, new forms of partnership seem to be emerging. These are multi-partite and consensual. To some extent their broad composition is redolent of the multi-partite bodies formed by the Manpower Services Commission, though the private sector and the trade unions play no direct role. However they have a much stronger executive role within programme management. Whether these programme management bodies will offer models for future governance is unclear.

## References

ASCETT (1996) *Annual Report*, Advisory Scottish Council for Education and Training Targets, Glasgow.

Ainley, P. and Corney, M. (1990) *Training for the Future – The Rise and Fall of the Manpower Services Commission*, London: Cassell.

Bastiani, J. (1993) 'Parents as Partners: Genuine Progress or Empty Rhetoric?', in P. Munn (ed.) *Parents and Schools – Customers, Managers or Partners?*, London: Routledge.

Benn, C. and Fairley, J. (eds) (1986) *Challenging the Manpower Services Commission*, London: Pluto Press.

Brown, A., McCrone, D. and Paterson, L. (1996) *Politics and Society in Scotland*, Basingstoke and London: Macmillan.

Brown, A. and Fairley, J. (eds) (1989) *The Manpower Services Commission in Scotland*, Edinburgh: Edinburgh University Press.

Burness, T. (1989) 'Further Education and the MSC', in A. Brown and J. Fairley (eds) *The Manpower Services Commission in Scotland*, Edinburgh: Edinburgh University Press.

Committee of Public Accounts (1990) *Fifteenth Report; Department of Employment: Provision of Training through Managing Agents*, HC 396 (2 May), London: HMSO.

Danson, M., Fairley, J., Lloyd, M.J. and Turok, I. (1996) *The Governance of the EU Structural Funds in Scotland*, seminar paper.

EIS/SCC (1996) *Education and a Scottish Parliament*, Educational Institute of Scotland and the Scottish Constitutional Convention.

Evans, B. (1992) *The Politics of the Training Market – From Manpower Services Commission to Training and Enterprise Councils*, London: Routledge.

Fairley, J. (1982) 'Industrial Training in Scotland', in H. Drucker and N. Drucker (eds) *The Yearbook of Scottish Government*, University of Edinburgh.

—— (1989) 'An Overview of the Development and Growth of the MSC in Scotland', in A. Brown and J. Fairley (eds) (1989) *The Manpower Services Commission in Scotland*, Edinburgh: Edinburgh University Press.

—— (1993) 'Negotiating Machinery Between the Social Partners in TVET in Britain', in *The Institutional Framework and Financing of Vocational Education and Training in Britain – Some Current Issues*, Scottish Local Authorities Management Centre, Glasgow: University of Strathclyde, August 1993.

—— (1995) 'Training Strategy in Scotland – Co-ordinating the Sectoral and Local Dimensions', *Regional Studies* 29 (8): 779–84.

—— (1996a) 'Vocational Education and Training in Scotland – Towards a Strategic Approach?', *Scottish Educational Review* 28 (1): 50–60.

—— (1996b) 'Scotland's New Local Authorities and Economic Development', *Scottish Affairs* 15 (Spring): 101–22.

Fairley, J. and Lloyd, M. (1995) 'Economic Development and Training in Scotland – The Roles of Scottish Enterprise, Highlands and Islands Enterprise and the Local Enterprise Companies', *Scottish Affairs*, June–July 1995.

Fairley, J. and Paterson, L. (1991) 'The Reform of Vocational Education and Training', *Scottish Educational Review* 23: 68–77.

FSB (1996) *The Enterprise Network in Scotland – a Survey of Members' Opinions*, Federation of Small Businesses, Glasgow.

Finlay, I. (1996) *Bridges or Battlements? Current Relationships between Colleges, Schools and Education Authorities*, Scottish School of Further Education, Glasgow: University of Strathclyde.

Finn, D. (1987) *Training Without Jobs; New Deals and Broken Promises*, Basingstoke and London: Macmillan.

Gleeson, D. (1989) *The Paradox of Training – Making Progress out of Crisis*, Milton Keynes: Open University Press.

Harvie, C. (1994) *Scotland and Nationalism – Scottish Society and Politics 1707–1994*, London: Routledge.

Humes, W. (1994) 'Policy and Management: mending the future,' in Humes, W. and Mackenzie, M. *The Management of Educational Policy: Scottish Perspectives*, Harlow: Longman.

Jackson, M. (1986) 'A Seat at the Table?', in C. Benn and J. Fairley (eds) *Challenging the Manpower Services Commission*, London: Pluto Press.

Leech, M. (1994) 'Management of Policy in Further Education', in W. Humes and M. MacKenzie (eds) *The Management of Educational Policy – Scottish Perspectives*, Harlow, Essex: Longman.

Liberal Democrat Party (1996) *Investing in Scotland's Future, An Educational Policy for Scotland*, Scottish Liberal Democrats, November 1996.

Maxwell, S. (1989) 'The MSC and the Voluntary Sector', in A. Brown and J. Fairley (eds) *The Manpower Services Commission in Scotland*, Edinburgh: Edinburgh University Press.

Osborne, D. and Gaebler, T. (1993) *Reinventing Government – How the Entrepreneurial Spirit is Transforming the Public Sector*, Reading, MA: Addison-Wesley.

Paterson, L. (1994) *The Autonomy of Modern Scotland*, Edinburgh: Edinburgh University Press.

Perry, P.J.C. (1976) *The Evolution of British Manpower Policy*, BACIE, London.

Pignatelli, F. (1994) 'Market Models and Managerialism in Education', in W. Humes and M. MacKenzie (eds) *The Management of Educational Policy – Scottish Perspectives*, Harlow, Essex: Longman.

Raab, C. (1993) 'Parents and Schools: What Role for Education Authorities', in P. Munn (ed.) *Parents and Schools – Customers, Managers or Partners?*, London: Routledge.

Robertson, G. (1996) 'A Stakeholder Economy – the Need for Partnership', speech delivered on 11 October 1996.

Scottish Affairs Committee (1995) *The Operation of the Enterprise Agencies and the LECs*, HC 339 (23 March), London: HMSO.

SNP (1992) *Industry Policy*, Scottish National Party, Edinburgh.

—— (1996) *Programme for Government*, Scottish National Party, Edinburgh.

Scottish Office (1996) *Policy and Financial Management Reviews of Scottish Enterprise and Highlands and Islands Enterprise, Prior Options Study*, 2 vols, London: HMSO.

Senker, P. (1992) *Industrial Training in a Cold Climate*, Aldershot: Avebury.

Speirs, B. (1989) 'The MSC in Scotland – The STUC View', in A. Brown and J. Fairley (eds) *The Manpower Services Commission in Scotland*, Edinburgh: Edinburgh University Press.

STUC (1996) *Consultation Paper – Beyond Enterprise: Shaping the Future for Economic Development and Training in Scotland*, Edinburgh: Scottish Trades Union Congress.

TUC (1995) *Modern Apprenticeship – A Negotiator's Guide*, Trades Union Congress, London.

Wright, J. (1989) 'The MSC as Seen by an Industrial Training Manager', in A. Brown and J. Fairley (eds) *The Manpower Services Commission in Scotland*, Edinburgh: Edinburgh University Press.

# 3

# A CONSENSUS APPROACH TO POLICY-MAKING

## The case of the Republic of Ireland

*Jim Gleeson*

## Introduction

There is a growing realisation in Ireland of the need to actively involve the social partners in the quest for an adequate response to the problem of social exclusion. This has resulted in the development of the policy of social consensus or partnership which underlies key government programmes for economic and social progress since 1987 and has come to be recognised, in the words of the Chairperson of the National Economic and Social Forum, Maureen Gaffney, as a 'model of social partnership which is the wonder of Europe' (she was speaking during a recent television discussion on the need to work to end social exclusion).

The National Education Convention (NEC), held in Dublin Castle in October 1993, has aroused considerable international interest because of its use of the strategy of consensus seeking in the development of education policy in the lead-up to the publication of the Education White Paper, *Charting Our Education Future* (Ireland 1995) in which partnership is enshrined as one of five fundamental educational principles which should underpin our education system and the December 1997 Education Act. This external attention probably explains my invitation to write this chapter, given that the topic of vocational education and training has only recently come to prominence in the Republic of Ireland. Against that background, it is my intention to focus on general policy-making strategy in some detail, before addressing the particular issue under discussion.

This chapter places the development of the partnership and consensus approach to national policy-making in the context of Ireland's difficult economic situation during the 1980s. The adoption of such an approach ensured that the VET needs of disadvantaged groups received higher levels of attention than heretofore. The National Education Convention of 1993 is considered as an instance of partnership in action and the discourse of the Convention is examined along with that of the ensuing White Paper on Education. VET policy and provision are examined and some related issues are discussed.

## The overall context: a consensus approach to national policy-making

Oliver Cussen, Assistant Secretary at the Department of Education, speaking at a conference on 'The Implementation of Educational Policy' in September 1995, stated that:

> Over the past number of years education has come much more centre stage in a wider social and economic context. This is evidenced in the incorporation of education within major social development programmes. Examples of this are the Programme for Economic and Social Progress, the Programme for National Recovery, the Programme for Competitiveness and Work, two major reports from the National Economic and Social Council and a very recent OECD report.
>
> (Coolahan 1995: 46)

The three programmes referred to by Cussen derive from a partnership approach, the beginnings of which can be traced back to the Fianna Fail/Progressive Democrat coalition government of the mid-1980s and to the work of the National Economic and Social Council (NESC) around that time. The main task of the NESC is to provide a forum for discussion of the principles relating to the efficient development of the national economy and the achievement of social justice, and to advise the Government on their application. The membership of the Council is drawn from four main areas: organisations engaged in agriculture, the industry sector and the Irish Congress of Trade Unions each provide five members, while the government nominates some nine other persons (including a representative of the National Youth Council and the Secretaries of the Departments of Finance, Trade and Tourism, and Enterprise and Employment).

Between 1980 and 1985 unemployment rates doubled from about 10 per cent to 20 per cent. Ryan commented that:

> The problems are more easily stated than solved. For example, if one takes nations such as Britain and West Germany, these have static population structures in which the numbers dying and being born are roughly equivalent, or in which the numbers retiring and entering the job market are roughly equal. Yet both have massive

unemployment problems. In Ireland, the birth rate (20.4 per 1,000 population) is more than double the death rate (9.4 per 1,000) and the numbers annually coming on the job market more than double the number of those retiring. This imbalance will continue at least to the end of the century. Those seeking jobs in the year 2000 are already born; there are 72,000 one-year-olds, more than double the number of forty-eight-year-olds, the potential retirement group seventeen years from now. Unless Ireland creates some 35,000 new jobs annually (highly unlikely) the unemployment figures will continue to grow.

(Ryan 1985: 3)

The NESC (1986) report, *A Strategy for Development 1986–1990*, set out the principles that should inform a response to our economic and social problems, namely that it was 'possible to simultaneously address the twin problems of mass unemployment and chronic fiscal imbalance through … an integral medium term strategy … which must command widespread acceptance throughout society if it is to be successful'. This strategy contained four elements: an integrated macro-economic policy; fundamental reform of the tax structure; the progressive removal of major inequities in society; a set of improved long-term development policies.

The first programme to result from the adoption of this approach, the *Programme for National Recovery* (PNR), opens with the following statement:

The Government, the Irish Congress of Trade Unions, the Federated Union of Employers, the Confederation of Irish Industry, the Construction Industry Federation, the Irish Farmers' Association, Macra na Feirme and the Irish Co-operative Organisation Society, *conscious of the grave state of our economic and social life*, have agreed on this Programme to seek to regenerate our economy and improve the social equity of our society through their combined efforts.

(Ireland 1987: 5; my emphasis)

Provision was made in the final section of the PNR for the establishment of a Central Review Committee, chaired by the Department of the Taoiseach and reporting to the government and the other parties of the Programme, to review and monitor progress in implementing the Programme. This Committee has played a most important role in the survival of the partnership strategy over ten years.

It should be acknowledged that the particularly good relationship which Charles J. Haughey, leader of Fianna Fail and the Taoiseach of the day, enjoyed with the Trade Union movement was a significant factor in the establishment of this 'consensus' strategy. In his introduction to the aptly named Programme for Economic and Social Progress (PESP), which succeeded the PNR, Haughey said 'In the PNR and the PESP we have fundamentally changed our approach to managing our affairs. Partnership between all the interests in our society is now the way forward' (Ireland 1991: 5).

The 'consensus' approach has remained in place throughout the intervening years. It is claimed in the National Development Plan that the progress achieved under the PNR had:

> stimulated significant economic and social progress. That progress confirmed the desirability of continuing the process of partnership between the Government and the social partners. ... The Government have accepted the Irish Congress of Trade Unions' proposal to adopt a long-term strategy for the development of this country over the next decade. The employer and farmer organisations have agreed to this approach.
>
> (Ireland 1994b: 7)

The second such programme (the PESP) had a broader base than the PNR in that submissions on the new programme were also received by the government from a number of other organisations including the National Youth Council, the Conference of Major Religious Superiors, the Catholic Social Service Conference, the Simon Community, the Housing Centre, the Irish Tourist Industry Confederation, the National Parents' Council and the Combat Poverty Agency. In the case of the third programme (Ireland 1994a), submissions were received from the same groups as before with the addition of the Irish National Organisation for the Unemployed (INOU), a developing organisation which has been seeking a more central role in the negotiation of the next programme.

The Fianna Fail/Labour coalition government, negotiated in 1993, based its *Programme for a Partnership Government*, on the principle that:

> the key to our whole approach will be to develop a strong sense of partnership, not only in terms of political structures but throughout the economy, our society and our community – a partnership that will be dynamic and creative, and geared towards confronting the major challenges that lie ahead of us. ... Achievement of our aims will be accomplished by broad social consensus, social solidarity, local initiative, openness and integrity, and the highest level of democratic participation.
>
> (Fianna Fail/Labour 1993: 1)

As an extension of its partnership policy, this government announced its intention to establish the National Economic and Social Forum under an independent chairperson and with its own secretariat:

The Forum will contribute to the formation of a national consensus on major issues of economic and social policy, and to the development of new initiatives to tackle unemployment. The Forum will have representatives from all the Social Partners, and in addition, representatives of women's organisations, groups representing the unemployed, the disadvantaged and people with a disability. ... The Social Partners and the Government will take account in their deliberations and in negotiating future economic programmes of the views expressed and positions agreed upon by the Forum.

(Fianna Fail/Labour 1993: 9)

The strategy of consensus through partnership was also used in the preparation of *The National Development Plan: 1994–99* which was submitted to the European Community as 'a plan for employment'. The central objective of the Plan is 'to ensure the best long-term return for the economy by increasing output, economic potential and long-term jobs. It is further designed to reintegrate the long-term unemployed and those at risk of becoming so into the economic mainstream' (Ireland 1994b: 7). As in the case of the various programmes discussed above, the preparation of the National Plan involved a very extensive process of consultation involving seven Sub-regional Review Committees (which included representatives of the local authorities, social partners and government departments) as well as the social partner organisations represented on the Central Review Committee of the PESP, the Chambers of Commerce of Ireland and the Council for the Status of Women.

When one considers the education and training measures in the PNR, PESP and PCW, what emerges is that these programmes are remarkable for their specificity, consisting as they do of piecemeal concessions such as increased resources for staffing, transport, building and so on. While all such concessions are very welcome to the hard-pressed school managers, principals, parents and teachers, they are hardly the stuff of critical reappraisal of the culture and values of an education system. The approach adopted suggests that the technical interest, as described in Carr and Kemmis (1986), is dominant.

As already noted, there is a growing consensus in Ireland regarding the need to balance supply and demand and tackle disadvantage. Certain influential members of government, both elected and administrative, have worked to bring this about over the years. The development of a National Anti-Poverty Strategy (NAPS) is a case in point. This proposed, for example, that the implementation of the 1994 Strategic Management Initiative should be audited, in order to 'poverty proof' its approach to the achievement of quality public service. Another implication of this growing concern with inequity has been the concern to offset the increasing proportion of education funding going to third level education by allocating additional investment in 'curative' initiatives such as Youthreach, the Leaving Certificate Applied, Early Start, the Vocational Training Opportunity Scheme and others.

The Consultation Paper on Institutional Mechanisms to support the NAPS explains its rationale in terms of ensuring that 'the issue of reducing poverty and social exclusion is firmly on the agenda of all government departments and agencies, and that there is appropriate coordination across and between departments on policy in this area' (Inter-Departmental Policy Committee 1995a: 1). It was recognised that 'the introduction and implementation of a NAPS ... may require a re-ordering of some government spending priorities, with increases in expenditure in some areas being compensated for by reductions in other areas' (Inter-Departmental Policy Committee 1995b: 29).

The NAPS received 241 submissions in response to its consultation on related strategic issues. Educational disadvantage was identified as the single most important issue to be addressed. 'Although less than 10 per cent of organisations and individuals making submissions could be specifically identified as having an interest in the area of education, almost 50 per cent of submissions raised education as a priority policy area. ... Submissions emphasised and re-emphasised the key role which education has to play in combating poverty and the links between educational disadvantage and social exclusion' (Inter-Departmental Policy Committee 1995c: 6, 20). While the new government which came into office in 1997 has not formally adopted the NAPS in its *Programme for Government*, the strategy is being implemented by most departments at this time. The new government has decided against the Regional Education Boards as proposed in the White Paper where their potential to promote partnership at local level was one of their perceived selling points.

The director of the NESC believes that 'Ireland's long-run pattern of policy-making and particularly our recent development of wide-ranging negotiated programmes, leaves us relatively well placed to develop the sorts of decision-making systems and institutions which are likely to be most effective in the 21st century' (O'Donnell 1995: 29). He argues that, with the demise of post-war Keynesian models of consensus and the resulting reduction in state dominance in the determination of policy, two changes are noticeable:

- the increase in the role of regional and local government in economic management;
- the move towards greater collaboration between the state, state agencies and organisations which represent those most affected by policy.

The members of the Central Review Committee worked intensively during 1996 as they attempted to put a programme in place to succeed the

PCW, which expired on 31 December 1996. Padraig Yeates, Industry and Employment correspondent at the *Irish Times*, under the heading 'Poor prospects for national pay deal', reported on 15 March 1996 that 'Since 1987 wages are up in real terms by about 1 per cent, and few unions see much value in another national pay agreement'. The Department of Finance and the Department of Enterprise and Employment were the key government departments involved in the discussions which finalised the new programme, known as Partnership 2000. The General Secretary of the Irish Congress of Trade Unions, Peter Cassells summed up the challenge:

> The last three agreements have served the country well and brought some benefits to working people and their families. But at this stage of the process it is clear that the process of social partnership either develops or it dies. It can be developed by deepening democratic content through real partnership at company level and by widening the scope through the inclusion of more flexible systems of rewards, like profit sharing.
>
> *(Irish Times*, 27 September 1996: 1)

Prior to the publication of the new programme, the NESC published its *Strategy into the 21st Century* report. It recognised that:

> Successful implementation (of the partnership process) is dependent on effective and extensive participation in social partnership and the monitoring of progress in negotiated programmes. Participation is still unevenly developed and the monitoring of progress has received little attention ... the achievements of national social partnership are hugely qualified by the continuing problem of long-term unemployment and social exclusion.
>
> (NESC 1996: 65)

The Council believes that the social partnership must be deepened and widened and that a wider distribution of the benefits of social partnership and of the fruits of growth as well as greater participation in policy formulation and implementation.

O'Toole (1997) reports on an interview with Carolann Duggan, a member of the Socialist Workers Party (SWP) who contested the presidency and vice-presidency of SIPTU, the largest trade union in Ireland during 1997. While not elected, she performed creditably in both elections. Duggan claims that:

> her motivation is simply to be a voice for the groundswell of opposition which has built up against Partnership 2000 and what she calls the so-called Celtic Tiger economy. ... She objects to the use of the word 'partnership' in the agreement. 'In any workplace I know

the workers are not in partnership with their employers. ... They live in a different world and don't live under the same pressure as working people'. ... She is dismissive of the collective wisdom that less industrial conflict and greater cooperation between management and unions have benefited the Irish economy. 'The compromise has been on our side all the time.'

Unlike its predecessors, the Partnership 2000 agreement contains no reference to the formal VET sector, other than the reference to the 'deepening of business–education linkages and co-operation through the shaping of curriculum and resources as appropriate' (Ireland 1996b: 23). The priorities in the programme are said to reflect those of the Status of People with Disabilities, the Task Force on the Travelling Community, the Review Body on Special Education and the deliberations of the NAPS theme group on educational disadvantage, as well as the recommendations of the NESC and the NESF. The focus in this programme is on the marginalised: non-standard applicants for third level education; early school leavers to be provided for in consultation with the relevant partners and with the Ministries of Health and Justice; early interventions at pre-school and primary levels, the expansion of Youthreach and the second chance VTOS programme, Traveller education and the Youth Service. When one considers the various programmes developed using the partnership approach, there is a clearly discernible pattern. Whereas the role of main-stream formal education in relation to VET is central in the early programmes (under the chapter heading 'Social Reform in the PESP and under Social Equity in the PCW') the most recent Partnership 2000 programme deals with the non-formal education sector only (this time under the heading of Action for Social Exclusion), presumably on the premise that the desirable developments in the formal sector have been put in place.

The twin-track approach of economic and social regeneration is also enshrined in the recently published European White Paper on Education and Training, where two of the five objectives include the combating of exclusion and equal treatment for capital investment and investment in training. It is recognised that 'the essential aim of education and training has always been personal development and the successful integration of Europeans into society through the sharing of common values, the passing on of cultural heritage and the teaching of self-reliance' (European Commission 1995: 3).

## Education policy-making: the National Education Convention

The scale of developments in relation to Irish education policy during the 1990s has been greater than at any time since independence: the report of the OECD Examiners (1991); the report of the Industrial Review Policy Group (Ireland 1992a); the Education Green Paper (Ireland 1992b); the 1993 National Education Convention; the publication of the report on the Convention (Coolahan 1994); the Education White Paper (Ireland 1995) – all culminating in the December 1997 Education Act.

The partnership approach was first put forward by Gemma Hussey, Minister for Education, in 1983 when she adopted the principles of partici-pation and consultation in relation to the establishment of the Curriculum and Examinations Board. The Special Ministerial Adviser of the day, John Harris comments 'As this (consultative) approach to policy formulation was relatively novel, in some of the consultations the working groups met with scepticism or suspicion from the parties consulted' (Mulcahy and O'Sullivan 1989: 17). The Education Green Paper, published in 1985, on the theme of establishing regional structures, was called *Partners in Education* (Ireland 1985) – a title which was 'indicative of the new approach to broadening the debate on major issues of policies and drawing more of the stakeholders into that debate' (McGuinness 1995; unpublished paper). Notwithstanding Hussey's efforts, the OECD Examiners report on Ireland found that:

> one of the missing or under-developed links in the curriculum-planning and decision-making process is the participation of the social partners. ... Their participation would also be a means whereby the current preoccupation with book and verbal knowledge accompanied by instructional modes of teaching and regurgitative practices in assessment and examinations should be reduced.
>
> (OECD 1991: 75)

The influence of the OECD in recent Irish education has been very signif-icant. Its 1965 report, with the significant title, *Investment in Education*, highlighted some of the more obvious weaknesses and inequalities in the system at that time and set the agenda for many of the developments which took place subsequently. The main preoccupation during the expansionary period up to the end of the 1980s was with responding to the increased numbers of students, particularly at second level. It was during this period also that school Boards of Management, with parent and teacher representa-tion, were introduced and the National Parents' Councils at primary and post-primary were officially established.

The 1992 Green Paper, *Education for a Changing World* (Ireland 1992b), proposed quite a fundamental reform of the system, centred around the promotion of what appear to be internationally accepted principles such as equality, partnership, quality, accountability, transparency, democracy, devo-lution and the promotion of social and economic well-being. Consultative regional meetings, seminars, conferences and symposia were a structured part of the ensuing debate. Some 1,000 responses to the Green Paper had been received at the Department of Education by April 1993 when the Minister for Education – the first Labour party member to hold that office in the history of the state – stated in her John Marcus O'Sullivan public lecture that:

> A common thread runs through many of these submissions which is variously expressed as a trenchant criticism of the absence of a coherent philosophy in the Green Paper. Alternatively, where such a philosophy is found to be present, a vigorous resistance to the tenets of such a philosophy is expressed. In short, various groups find the Green Paper devoid of philosophy or possessed of an implicit philosophy which in some way narrows or even perverts the true aims of education.
>
> (Breathnach 1994: 6)

The minister's remarks refer to the strong negative reaction to what was perceived as a quasi-Thatcherite, market-led emphasis in the Green Paper, as exemplified by the importance ascribed to the proposed new subject 'Technology and Enterprise' and in the reference to the school principal – even in the case of small, rural, one- or two-teacher primary schools – as Chief Executive. The background documentation to the Report of the Industrial Policy Review Group revealed a similar mentality, with the intro- duction of 'free' secondary education after 1966 being seen in terms of 'the provision of an increased range of heavily-subsidised education products to potential consumers' (Roche and Tansey 1992: 12).

The minister in the course of the same lecture, emphasised the impor- tance of partnership:

> implicit in all of these assumptions is an immense unquestioning faith in the power of education to bring about an improvement in social order and morality. ... Central to the continuing work of this huge and complex system is the notion of partnership – partnership between the child and the educator and the parent, between the school and the community, between the institutions of education and the development needs of society.
>
> (Breathnach 1994: 4)

The idea for the National Education Convention arose, therefore, out of the felt need to work towards consensus in relation to an underlying philos- ophy, on the grounds that 'if we do not achieve a consensual view of a coherent philosophic framework in our debate towards framing the White Paper, there is no magic formula which will provide a philosophy when we come to proposing the Bill' (Breathnach 1994: 10).

This is the background against which the National Education Convention took place in Dublin Castle over a period of nine days in October 1993. The minister had decided that the Convention should be organised independently of the Department of Education. Professor John Coolahan, who had played an important advisory role in relation to the preparation of the Green Paper, was nominated by the minister to act as Secretary General to the Convention. Coolahan, whose own base is in the History of Education, selected a Secretariat of six academics, of whom four were from a sociology background, to assist him. The minister also appointed a chairperson who presided over the Convention itself.

Some forty-two bodies,[1] from a diversity of backgrounds, participated in the Convention.

> These comprised those organisations directly and centrally involved in the education process and included representatives of patrons/owners of schools; managerial organisations; school management organisations; teacher unions; National Parents' Councils; Heads of Universities and Directors of Higher Education Institutions, curriculum and assessment organisations. Other organisations less closely associated with the system such as the social partners, farming and trade union and employer organisations and cultural groups also attended.
>
> (McGuinness 1995; unpublished paper)

The Union of Students of Ireland, which normally represents the interests of third level students, spoke on behalf of all school-goers. A full listing of the organisations represented at the Convention is presented as Appendix 3.1. Each organisation made a formal presentation during its allotted time (ranging from 15–30 minutes) in which it outlined its responses to the proposals for change and took questions from the Secretariat on matters arising. During the second week of the Convention specific issues were debated at some length during concurrent group discussion sessions: these included the governance and internal management of schools; curriculum issues; local education structures; the role of the Department of Education and of the Inspectorate and school rationalisation. A member of the Secretariat chaired each group discussion and a rapporteur recorded the proceedings. Two particularly contentious issues were further discussed at special round-table sessions during the following months: regional structures and the constitution of school management boards.

It is important to place the Convention in context, in order to appreciate the significance of this novel initiative. The majority of Irish schools are privately owned and managed but publicly funded. The Department of Education has been so busily engaged in day-to-day management activities such as the sanctioning and recognition of schools, approving staffing ratios, providing funding and determining curriculum and assessment policies, that its main function of developing policy proposals and conducting research and evaluation in relation to the implementation of policy has been largely ignored until very recently. Yet, as the OECD Examiners (1991: 36ff.) pointed out, Irish schools have enjoyed a great deal of autonomy in relation to matters such as school ethos, admission policy, selection of staff, organisation of the curriculum and grouping of students because we did not have intermediate structures operating at a level between the Department and the individual schools. Indeed, a recent OECD report (1995) identifies Ireland as the member country where schools have most autonomy in decision-making.

Professor Michael Connolly, looking at the Convention from the perspective of the Chair of Public Policy and Management at the University of Ulster, comments that:

> one striking feature from the perspective of the UK is to note how open the process in the Republic has been. The notion of a current member of the British Cabinet convening a meeting involving academics, trade unionists and other interested and knowledgeable people to determine the makeup of educational reform is the stuff of fantasy. Of course, the Republic of Ireland has always been a more corporate polity than the UK and its relatively smaller size makes such activities easier to manage. But the contrast remains stark. ... One result is that there really was a genuine debate on education, unlike the great debate in Britain which was characterised by sound and fury and little meeting of minds. ... The process of involving the key actors in determining the issues and the solutions has important implications for implementation. Agreement undoubtedly enhances the likelihood of successful implementation. The Background Paper uses an eloquent phrase – 'a partnership of effort' – in the context of implementation.
>
> (Connolly 1994: 19)

Connolly expresses surprise that issues of management and organisation were so dominant at the expense of curriculum, which was just passed on to the National Council for Curriculum and Assessment.

The NEC model is regarded as highly successful in Ireland. For instance, during a recent television discussion Liz McManus, Democratic Left TD and spokesperson, suggested that it was a suitable model for the achievement of progress on what has been a hugely controversial issue in Ireland, namely abortion – this against the background of two divisive referenda which have arguably raised more issues than they solved.

## The discourse of partnership

The term 'stakeholder', so commonly used in some countries, is very seldom used in the context of Irish education. Analysis of the verbatim record of the National Education Convention reveals that, during the recorded exchanges, the term was used on only three occasions and by the same participant on each occasion. This participant (the main spokesperson for the National Parents' Council – Primary) used it interchangeably with 'partner', a term which featured very frequently during her presentation: 'We feel that is a responsibility which must be shared on a partnership basis by all the stake-holders in the school' (Irish Stenographers: Day 1, p. 44). The subsequent White Paper (Ireland 1995) does not include a single usage of the term 'stakeholder'.

The negative reaction to the perceived 'enterprise culture' of the Green Paper may help to explain the absence of stakeholder-type language at the Convention and in the White Paper. The comments of McCormack, repre-senting the Conference of Religious in Ireland (CORI), the 'liberal wing' of the Catholic Church in Ireland, are indicative of this reaction: 'What is totally missing from the Green Paper is any explication of the vision of society and model of development on which it is based. ... In particular the language of the introduction seems excessively consumerist with concepts like competition given a very strong emphasis' (McCormack 1992: 27).

My analysis of the record of the Convention reveals that the terms 'part-ners' and/or 'partnership' were used on some 256 occasions, in a variety of senses, referring *inter alia* to the *Programme for Government*; the education and/or social partners; the participants in the Convention; partnership with local business, and so on. Closer scrutiny reveals that the minister herself was the most persistent user, followed by members of the Secretariat, and the Education Officer of the OECD, Professor Skilbeck, who attended for three days. The minister pointedly addressed the attendance at the opening ceremony as 'Partners in education' and went on to state that the Convention:

> marks a major change in the way education policy is to be formu-lated for the next generation of pupils in Ireland. It arises from our commitment to partnership as expressed in the *Programme for a Partnership Government* [which] ... pledges us to commit ourselves to democracy, to devolution and openness, to a genuine and mean-ingful role for all partners in education and to a focusing of resources towards disadvantaged areas and groups.
>
> (Irish Stenographers: Day 1, p. 4)

Her concluding address on the final day of the Convention gave a similar message: 'And at the close of this Convention you can all, partners in education, feel satisfaction and pride that you have played your full part in helping me shape the future of Irish education. Partners in education I congratulate you' (Day 7, p.116).

Of the delegations presenting at the Convention, the parents made most frequent use of the term 'partnership', sending a clear 'political' message:

> Firstly, we look to a formal acknowledgement, both of the individual interest of parents in their child's schooling, and also the collective interest of parents, as stakeholders and partners in the schools' educational task ... either the ethos of partnership prevails in the structure of Boards or it does not. There cannot be partnership and dominance ... the concept of partnership needs to be built into the process of national decision-making, underpinned by legislative structures.
>
> (Irish Stenographers: Day 1, p. 36)

It is significant to note that the school management bodies and the Teacher Unions were sparing in their usage of the concept at the Convention, as were the other 'special interest' groups represented.

The reaction of Connolly is of interest here:

> In looking at the debate on structures in the Report one is struck both by how up to date it is in certain respects but also by how old-fashioned it is. The arguments about delegation are not only sensible and appropriate but also the sorts of argument that are heard in many areas of administrative reform. But, while in some respects implicit, notions of the split between purchaser/provider did not rate a mention. Yet these notions are more appropriate in education than in say the health service in the UK.
>
> (Connolly 1994: 20)

Is there a certain suggestion here that the emphasis on partnership has resulted in the neglect of the particular concerns of certain interest groups?

The Education White Paper (Ireland 1995) includes some sixty-six references to 'partners/partnership'; in fact partnership is one of the five basic principles adopted in the White Paper along with pluralism, equality, quality and accountability. In establishing partnership as one of the five fundamental principles of Irish education, there is an acknowledgement that the learner is at the centre of the educational process, and the other principal participants are collectively referred to as:

> the partners in education – parents, patrons/trustees/owners/governors, management bodies, teachers, the local community and the State. Other participants, including the social partners, businesses

and the professions, should also be recognised as having legitimate interests in the system. Effective partnership involves active co-operation among those directly involved in the provision of education and the anchoring of educational institutions and structures in the wider communities they serve.

(Ireland 1995: 7)

In the context of vocational education and training, the White Paper identifies:

a need for a more cohesive approach to the development of all vocational education and training to maximise the benefit to students, society and the economy. ... This will take place in the context of the new organisational arrangements set out in this White Paper, including the establishment of the Further Education Authority and the clarification of the respective roles of the Department of Education and the Department of Enterprise and Employment.

(Ireland 1995: 73)

The contrast between the uses of the terms 'partnership' and 'stakeholder' in recent debates on education in Ireland is most interesting. The concept stakeholder is used in two different senses with the narrow definition meaning 'those groups who are vital to the survival and success of the function' and the broader one including 'any group or individual who can affect or is affected by the function' (Garavan 1995: 11). Equally, there are levels of partnership, as indicated in the quotation from the White Paper given earlier. As Garavan reminds us, 'power is a key issue in any consideration of stakeholder influences' (ibid.). On the other hand, the discourse of partnership puts the emphasis on the active participation of equals in a collaborative way.

## Vocational education and training policy and practice

The population of the Republic of Ireland is approximately 3.5 million with a density of 50 per square kilometre. Its age profile (Clancy *et al.* 1995: 49) is atypical in that it has the highest proportion of 0–14 and 15–44 year olds in Western Europe. The OECD Examiners pointed out that Ireland:

is characterised by its youthfulness. Over half the population is under 25, and 30.5 per cent is under 15. ... Apart from Australia and Turkey, Ireland is the only OECD country to have experienced a rising birth-rate until very recently ... thus as school enrolments were on the decrease almost everywhere else, enrolments in Ireland were swiftly increasing, and the pressure on resources was almost unsustainable.

(OECD 1991: 13)

Education expenditure rose from 16 per cent of total government expenditure in 1965 to 20 per cent in 1993, and from 3.2 per cent of GNP in 1965 to 6.5 per cent in 1992. While these figures are around the OECD average, Irish expenditure per pupil is much lower than in other member countries (see OECD 1995: 73).

Participation rates in post-compulsory education had risen to 78 per cent by 1994 (85 per cent for young women) – this is above the OECD average. 'The target is for at least a 90 per cent completion rate by the end of the 1990s' (Ireland 1995: 50). In 1994, 38 per cent of all school-leavers entered higher education. This proportion will approach 50 per cent by the year 2000 as the size of the age cohort falls and more places are provided.

While we had the lowest working population (in percentage terms) in the EU, unemployment rose steadily in Ireland through the 1980s, reaching 19 per cent in 1988, second only to Spain (see Commission of the European Communities 1989: 14). It has recently dropped back below 300,000 and stands currently at 10 per cent.[2]

The OECD (1995: 47ff.) draws attention to some aspects of the Irish situation which are of particular relevance to the issue of vocational education and training (VET).

- Our students finish second level schooling at 17, which is some two years younger than in most member states, and many complete university at 20 having taken three-year degree courses.
- The OECD reported that 'there do not appear to be specific skill shortages' partly because employers always have the option of hiring workers home from the traditional migratory destination in neighbouring Britain.
- Levels of educational attainment on the part of young Irish adults (25–34 years of age) were significantly less than the OECD average for 1991, but these figures do not reflect the improvements in educational attainments that have taken place recently.
- The opportunities for education are very unevenly distributed across Irish society (see, for example, Clancy 1995 and the publications of CORI).[3]
- While the proportion of Irish students following vocational education type courses (as defined by the OECD) is only 20 per cent – it is often 50 per cent or more in other European countries – the uptake of scientific, technical and applied linguistic subjects has been rising steadily (Lynch 1992: 13ff.) and there has been a dramatic rise in participation rates in vocationally oriented Post-Leaving Certificate Courses (PLCs) over the past five years. There are currently some 20,000 participants in PLCs per year out of an annual year cohort of approximately 65,000; the number of participants in 1989 was 12,000.

But the success of the Celtic Tiger is resulting in some changes. Notwithstanding what the OECD reported in 1995 about our skill requirements, certain initiatives were launched by the Minister for Education in July 1997 which were designed to meet 'emerging and critical skills demands in the high-technology sector'. The press release went on to say that 'This initiative represents the government's immediate response to meeting the skills needs identified by high-technology companies who are concerned about the effect which the lack of suitably trained employees will have on their ability to expand'. An immediate capital investment of £5 million was made available for 1997, with the promise of further grants in coming years. The groundwork was done by a FORFAS[4] Skills Group and by a Steering Committee with representatives of the Departments of Enterprise and Employment, Finance, and Education working in conjunction with the third level education institutions. At the launch of the initiative the Minister for Education stated that he was 'committed to ensuring that our education system is to the fore in meeting the skills needs of our rapidly expanding economy'. The emphasis so far has been on computer science at undergraduate and postgraduate levels and on multilingual teleservices/telemarketing skills. On 9 October, the minister announced the establishment of a new industry/college initiative to jointly recruit and educate and train technicians. Further initiatives along these lines are promised from the joint education/industry Task Force under the heading 'Government committed to meeting skills needs of economy'.

The Secretary of the Department of Education, Noel Lindsay, speaking at an EU Conference on Education and Training, had raised the issue of a broad-based education versus a dual type approach as if this choice was being seriously considered within the Department (Crooks and O'Dwyer 1990: 20). The *Report of the Industrial Policy Review Group* (Ireland 1992a) advocated the adoption of the German dual system. NESC (1993: ch. 4) considered the adequacy of current vocational education and training policy in Ireland in comparison with Denmark and the Netherlands, two countries where it was being proposed to dispense with the dual system. The NESC study concluded that, while Ireland lags behind many European countries, particularly Denmark and the Netherlands, in its vocational education provision, 'this situation may also confer advantages if the opportunity is taken to draw on the experiences of other countries ... in building a system that is comprehensive and flexible' (1993: 128). The report concluded that:

> one of the most strikingly distinctive features of the Irish vocational education and training system from an international comparative perspective is the limited amount of structured training which occurs in the workplace and the peripheral role of employers in the education and training system.
>
> (NESC 1993: 222)

The Interim Curriculum and Examinations Board (1986: 33), now the National Council for Curriculum and Assessment (NCCA), which advises the minister in relation to the primary and post-primary curriculum, has consistently opposed the adoption of a dual-track approach, favouring instead the provision of a broad, general education. Their approach to post-compulsory education was adopted by the authors of the Green Paper, went unchallenged at the NEC – where 'there was a general commitment to a balanced holistic curriculum at second level' (Coolahan 1994: 73) – and was enshrined in the White Paper.

The Report on the NEC comments on the Green Paper's proposals in relation to senior cycle education, saying that for the:

> period of second level education, when utilitarian views might be expected to be most in evidence, [it] had advocated a comprehensive approach to curriculum rather than a dual system of academic and vocational education which is common in other European countries and had been proposed in the Culliton report.
>
> (Coolahan 1994: 75)

The reaction of the Irish Business and Employers' Confederation (IBEC) to this debate was quite significant. In its response to the Green Paper it referred to 'the phoney debate' around humanism versus utilitarianism and asserted that:

> Industry recognises that education serves a variety of purposes – social, economic and cultural – and that its effects are cumulative and long-term rather than immediate. It cannot therefore be planned, organised or directed merely in response to the transient demands of economic cycles or fashionable social philosophies. In the turbulent world of today, with fragile family and other social institutions, this consideration is all the more important: education becomes the main vehicle for maintaining and transmitting the basic values on which the cohesion of future societies depends.
>
> (IBEC 1993: 4)

In its recent policy statement, *Social Policy in a Competitive Economy*, IBEC adopts a similar position when it recognises that:

> close partnership within the education and training systems and between those systems and the economy are essential. ... In order to combat this problem, IBEC has emphasised the need to develop a broadly based education system on which more specialist knowledge and skills can be built at a later stage and as the need arises.
>
> (IBEC 1996: 21)

Based on an analysis of the verbatim account of the NEC, only two of the presenting agencies referred specifically to VET – the National Council for Vocational Awards and the Irish Vocational Education Association which is the umbrella body for the local Vocational Education Committees. This neglect is acknowledged in the Convention Report:

> The Secretariat is conscious that some important areas of education do not receive significant attention in its Report. Among such areas are vocational training [sic] and youth affairs. In this regard, however, the Secretariat draws attention to the significant report by the NESC (1993) for comprehensive treatment of the training area.
>
> (Coolahan 1994: 4)

This lack of attention reflects the reality that VET has not been a high priority issue in Ireland; for example, the presentation made by the Association of Principals of Vocational Schools and Community Colleges at the NEC explained that 'A Further Education sector was never established officially. It evolved in response to changing student needs and particularly the need of students to achieve high level qualifications for employment' while the Teachers' Union of Ireland presentation included reference to Post-Leaving Certificate courses as the 'twilight zone of Irish education'. While we have a burgeoning VET system at Post-Leaving Certificate level, one has to wonder about its future when the school-going population drops and accommodation at third level increases.

Sugrue (1995) points out that 'a very striking feature of the White Paper as a policy document is the extent to which it relies on and quotes extensively from the Convention Report'. The lack of attention to VET at the Convention is reflected in the paucity of direct NEC quotes in the relevant section of the White Paper, as against those sections dealing with issues such as governance and management. The White Paper (Ireland 1995: 71ff.) includes four points of particular importance for VET.

1    It emphasises the need to improve the working relationship between the ministries of Education and Enterprise and Employment 'in order to ensure a co-ordinated and focused approach at Government level ... it is essential that unnecessary overlap and duplication in provision is avoided and that policy making is co-ordinated on the basis of well defined roles.' The Department's 1996 publication, *Implementing the Agenda for Change*, refers to the on-going work on the 'clarification of the respective roles and responsibilities of the Departments ... in relation to vocational education and training' (Ireland 1996a: 35).

2　The proposal to establish a new Further Education Authority 'to provide a coherent national development framework, appropriate to the importance of vocational education and training (outside the third level sector) and adult and continuing education.' Some preparatory consultancy work has since been undertaken in this respect (ibid.).

3　The proposal to establish TEASTAS, the Irish National Certification Authority, in response to the felt need 'for a more coherent and effective system of certification for the non-university sector of higher education as well as the vocational training sector ... The Report of the NEC recorded widespread approval for such a unified national awards framework'. In 1996 we were told that this body had been established on 'an ad hoc basis and is working closely with various interests and existing certification bodies to establish a national qualifications framework and to advise on the appropriate legislative underpinning for the body'. By all accounts, progress on this front is slow.

4　The imminent introduction of the Leaving Certificate Applied Programme (LCA) was welcomed in the White Paper which stated that it 'will be fully integrated into the system for a certification of educational and training qualifications being developed by TEASTAS' (Ireland 1995: 53).

## Provision of VET

Those who leave school at or before the end of compulsory schooling are catered for by the Youthreach programme. Some 4,500 young people participated in this programme in 1996 and were paid a weekly allowance of IR£25 per week for 15–17 year olds, IR£32 per week for 17–18 year olds and IR£52.50 per week for 18+ year olds, along with meal and travel allowances. They had the option of taking NCVA Foundation Level and Level 1 courses and of moving further up the NCVA ladder. Responsibility for Youthreach is shared between FAS[5] and the Department of Education and the programme is sometimes provided by means of Community Training Workshops at FAS Training Centres. There are plans to provide an additional 1,000 Youthreach places during 1997–8.

The clear statement in the White Paper in relation to the Department of Education's primary responsibility for vocational education and training is to be welcomed in view of the ambivalence which has historically surrounded the respective roles of the Department of Labour/Enterprise and Employment *vis-à-vis* the Department of Education in relation to VET.

The following options are provided at the post-compulsory stage of mainstream education:

Transition Year (optional one-year enrichment programme)

Established Leaving Certificate (two-year programme)

Leaving Certificate Vocational (two-year programme)

Leaving Certificate Applied (two-year programme)

Post-Leaving Certificate Courses (one- or two-year programme)

*Figure 3.1*: Post-compulsory education options in the Republic of Ireland

*Established Leaving Certificate.*   The Established Leaving Certificate student normally takes seven from the menu of some thirty-one subjects with an option of Ordinary and Higher levels (as well as Foundation level in the case of Irish and Maths) in relation to each subject.

*Leaving Certificate Vocational.* The Leaving Certificate Vocational Programme (LCVP) student is required to take three work-related 'link modules' (Preparation for Work; Work Experience; Enterprise Education), Irish language, a continental language (this may be taken at Junior Certificate level), two subjects from a list of vocational subject groupings (either *Specialist* or *Services*) and at least one other subject from the prescribed list of subjects. An example of a *Specialist* grouping of subjects would be Accounting and Business Organisation or Engineering and Technical Drawing, while an example from the *Services* grouping would be Business Organisation along with any *Specialist* subject such as Construction Studies.

*Leaving Certificate Applied.*   The Leaving Certificate Applied (LCA) is a broadly based pre-vocational education programme, intended for young people who do not wish to transfer directly to third level education. It has been designed as a real alternative to the Established Leaving Certificate in terms of breadth and balance, curriculum integration and organisation, pedagogy, assessment and certification, student motivation, community involvement and general focus (Gleeson and Granville 1996). Now that participants in the non-formal VET sector (Youthreach, VTOS and Traveller Education Centres) are beginning to participate in the LCA, the suitability of the school-based programme for other audiences is coming under the microscope.

*Post-Leaving Certificate Courses.*   Post-Leaving Certificate Courses (PLCs) are aimed at those who have completed senior cycle education. 'Their objective is to meet the needs of the economy, to equip young people with the vocational and technological skills necessary for employment and progression to further education and training, and to foster innovation and adaptability in participants' (Ireland 1995: 73) and the focus is on technical knowledge, personal development and work experience.

The LCA is the newest and most innovative of the above programmes and raises some interesting questions about partnership in practice. While the 'ring-fenced' nature of the programme allows considerable freedom for innovation on the one hand, it increases the fear of stigmatisation[6] on the other hand. Other writers in this book (e.g. Bellis and Rau) have referred to the danger of 'ghettoisation' for participants in alternative, less academic school programmes. The issue of the recognition of the new award by employers and Further Education agencies (Gleeson and Granville 1996) is an example of partnership being put to the test. NESC (1993: 211ff.) suggested that 'the prospects for success of alternatives to the present general Leaving Certificate would be enhanced by linking such programmes, through structured and possibly exclusive routes, to further training and into the labour force'. There has not been any rush by the partners to implement the NESC suggestion to date. LCA students wishing to progress to further education and training may do so via a Post-Leaving Certificate Course (NCVA Level 2) which opens up certain possibilities in the non-university third level sector. However, the primary concern of the typical LCA participant is with the acceptability of her/his qualification to employers, including the state itself. The response to the NESC proposal for preferential treatment for participants in alternative programmes in relation to certain employment options raises serious questions about the partnership approach as applied to VET.

The LCA throws up a second critical issue in relation to the partnership approach to national policy-making. The largest Teacher Union at post-primary level has refused to implement the school-based assessment proposals which were an integral part of the programme as designed. As the Project Manager for the development of the LCA from 1993–5, I believe that this refusal is seriously curtailing the effectiveness of the programme. While the Irish Congress of Trade Unions has played a strategically important role in the achievement of a partnership approach to government at the macro level, here we find one of its strongest constituent unions unwilling to cooperate with a vital aspect of an initiative developed to address the needs of those most likely to experience the worst effects of inequality.

## Some concluding remarks

Certain native factors have contributed to the development of a partnership model of government in the Irish situation:

- Ireland's peculiar demography and difficult economic circumstances – as already noted, the PNR was born out of adversity – have resulted in a greater appreciation of the social dimension of the policy-making process.
- the leadership qualities of certain key political and administrative figures and sectional representatives have been vital in the evolution of this approach to policy making.
- the vagaries of a Proportional Representation electoral system, which has returned a series of coalition governments in which the Labour/Left dimension has played a critical role during most of the last ten years.

The principle of consensus is as universally acceptable as motherhood or apple-pie, yet the implementation of reform is always demanding and complex (see Carter and O'Neill 1995: ch. 6). While equity has been *adopted* as an over-riding principle in the Education White Paper, it is salutary to remember that this principle will be *implemented* within the framework of what Streeck and Schmitter (1985) refer to as 'self-interested collective action', a negotiated compromise between the various 'stakeholders' with their own agendas. The significance of political factors emerges strongly in the above paper. The 1997 General Election resulted in a change of government; policies such as the NAPS, the establishment of Regional Education Boards and the establishment of TEASTAS have been either shelved or had their implementation delayed. The previous minister's strong commitment to the partnership approach has been noted already, as has the reluctance of the traditional partners to employ the discourse of partnership at the National Education Convention. The existence of some political dissatisfaction from the Left and from within the Trade Union movement is evidence of perceived shortcomings in the implementation of partnership policies. At an ideological level our education system is highly competitive and individualistic (see Lynch 1989) with little opportunity for the voices of the disadvantaged to be heard in relation to policies that have served the educated classes well (see Hannan and Boyle 1987). The LCA presents particular challenges to partnership in relation to assessment and recognition and the treatment of these issues will be telling.

At the start of the NEC the Secretary General called for tolerance on the part of the educational partners in the interests of achieving agreement rather than discord on educational issues (Coolahan 1994: 224). Returning to this theme at the conclusion of the Convention, he observed that 'there has been an openness to the ideas of others. ... Instead of rigidity of set viewpoints, I think it is fair to say that there was a fluidity in the exchanges and interrelationships that were occurring' (1994: 236). Looking beyond the Convention itself, he stressed the importance of proceeding in a spirit of compromise: 'If everybody just holds to his/her own cherished positions and ignores the concerns of others, then we do not rise to our responsibility or the opportunities provided by the consultative process. The art of compromise is crucial to the social cement of healthy democracies' (1994: 233).

It is one thing to accept in principle the need for compromise. It is another thing to achieve it when real problems have to be resolved in a manner acceptable to the vested interests at the table. As noted earlier, the parent representatives at the NEC emphasised the attitude change required to make the partnership idea work at ground level. Peter Cassells, General Secretary of the Irish Congress of Trade Unions (RTE radio interview, 26 September 1996) suggested that, while the partnership model has worked well at central level, it has not transferred successfully to the local level. The recent decision of the present government not to proceed with the establishment of Regional Education Boards makes one wonder how the principle of partnership will be translated at regional and local level in the education system.

In his concluding observations, the General Secretary of the NEC said that 'ideas were on the move' (Coolahan 1994: 236). When one considers the outcomes of the Convention, it would appear that it worked best on the 'technical' and bureaucratic levels rather than on the philosophical, cultural and belief levels, focusing primarily as it did on issues to do with power and control (Gleeson 1996). The achievement of consensus in relation to an underlying philosophy – the original brief of the NEC – is a more complex undertaking than agreement about wage levels or budget allocations. To date, the partnership approach to the implementation of the White Paper policy proposals has involved the establishment of representative committees dealing with what are essentially technical and political issues such as School Accommodation Needs and the *implementation* of some new education programmes.

The international literature suggests some salutary lessons in relation to the consensus model. Apple warns against the use of the consensus-building approach within the context of the 'authoritarian populism' of the New Right in the United States on the grounds that:

> one of the major aims of a rightist restoration politics is to struggle in not one but many different arenas at the same time, not only in the economic sphere but also in education and elsewhere ... the common good is now to be regulated exclusively by the laws of the market. ... In essence the definitions of freedom and equality are no longer democratic but *commercial*.
>
> (Dale 1989: 6ff.)

The emergence of NAPS and the strong voice of champions of social justice such as CORI give cause for hope of a more democratic outcome in the case of Ireland.

Humes (1986: 96ff.) in his provocative study of the 'leadership class' in

Scottish education considers the Consultative Committee on the Curriculum (CCC) as an instance of democracy in action. He finds that this approach assumes a:

> consensus model of policy formulation and implementation in which the smooth running of the bureaucratic machine is a prime consideration. Whether such a model is conducive to the kind of independent, critical thinking which would seem to be a necessary pre-requisite of worthwhile educational reform is open to doubt ...
>
> (Humes 1986: 96ff.)

He goes on to highlight the reliance of the Secretary of State on the patronage system when it comes, for example, to the appointment of the members of the CCC. There is a body of opinion in Ireland that the operation of partnership in the context of a such a small country throws many of the same representatives together to such an extent that the resulting familiarity may not be to the advantage of those they represent.

While there has been a growing awareness in Ireland of the economic significance of high quality education and training, we have yet to give serious consideration to what Young refers to as 'the idea of a learning-led economy ... [which gives] priority to learning as a feature of society as a whole being a condition for a successful economy of the future' (1995: 144). Irish education and training policy has, in contrast, been economy-led (see, for example, O'Sullivan 1992). Referring to the 'crisis in post-compulsory education', particularly in Western Europe, Young argues that, since this crisis 'has its origins in the economy ... then any framework for assessing proposals for reconstruction cannot be education bound ... it has to be a framework that conceptualises education–economy relationships in the context of a view of society as a whole'. This line of thinking leads on to the concept of the 'learning society' where 'divisions are based not on wealth and property but on the distribution of knowledge and skill. According to such a view the wealth of a society is the skills and knowledge of its people' – *all* its people. It is this inclusiveness which Partnership 2000 espouses and which inspired the NAPS.

## Appendix 3.1: Bodies represented at the National Education Convention

1 Association of Chief Executive Officers of Vocational Educational Committees
2 Association of Community and Comprehensive Schools
3 Association of Managers of Catholic Secondary Schools/Joint Managerial Body for Second Level Schools

4 Association of Principals and Vice-Principals of Community and Comprehensive Schools
5 Association of Principals and Vice-Principals of Voluntary Secondary Schools
6 Association of Principals of Vocational Schools and Community Colleges
7 Association of Secondary Teachers of Ireland
8 Bord na Gaeilge (responsible for promoting the Irish language)
9 Campaign to Separate Church and State
10 Catholic Episcopal Commission for Education
11 Catholic Primary Schools Managers' Association
12 Church of Ireland Board of Education
13 Comhdhail Naisiunta na Gaeilge (Irish language organisation)
14 Committee of Heads of Irish Universities
15 Conference of Religious in Ireland
16 Council for the Status of Women
17 Council of Higher Education Directors
18 Department of Education
19 Educate Together
20 FAS (the National Industrial Training Authority)
21 Forum of People with Disabilities
22 Gaelscoileanna (Irish language primary schools group)
23 Higher Education Authority
24 Irish Business and Employers' Confederation
25 Irish Congress of Trade Unions
26 Irish Creamery Milk Suppliers' Association
27 Irish Farmers' Association
28 Irish Federation of University Teachers
29 Irish National Organisation of the Unemployed
30 Irish National Teachers' Organisation
31 Irish Vocational Education Association
32 National Council for Curriculum and Assessment
33 National Council for Educational Awards
34 National Council for Vocational Awards
35 National Parents' Council (Post-Primary)
36 National Parents' Council (Primary)
37 National Youth Council
38 Presidents of Colleges of Education
39 Secondary Education Committee
40 Teachers' Union of Ireland
41 The Arts Council
42 The National Association of Adult Education
43 The Special Education Review Committee
44 Union of Students of Ireland

The Department of Education was also represented and made its own presentation during the second week of the Convention.

## Notes

1 The official number of participating organisations is given as forty-two; when one counts the number of bodies making presentations it comes to forty-five.
2 See Clancy *et al*. (1995: 95) for a table which highlights the difficulty of getting agreement about unemployment figures.
3 Hannan *et al*. (1995: 336) draws attention to the 'sharp contrast between the returns to taking or not taking qualifications in Ireland and the UK. These differences in returns are consistent with the rapid increase in qualification levels in Ireland and the slow advance of qualifications in the UK during the 1980s. ... It seems most likely that the differences come from the side of the labour market'. Having highlighted the importance of programmes of transition and integration for early leavers they conclude that 'of the three countries (Ireland, Netherlands and the UK), Ireland is clearly the one with the least development of policies in regard to transition and integration' (1995: 340).
4 FORFAS is the policy advisory and coordination board for industrial development and science and technology in Ireland. It is the body in which the state's legal powers for industrial promotion and technology development have been vested.
5 The national Employment and Training Authority.
6 The programme came in for some rather negative discussion at the NEC, where the hope was expressed that 'since the course will not lead to formal vocational qualifications and the course's certificands may only progress to limited courses of post-secondary education, there is a distinct danger that it will be seen as a "soft-option" track and of limited value by students' (Coolahan 1994: 76).

## References

Association of Principals of Vocational Schools and Community Colleges (1994) Submission to the National Education Convention, National Archives, Dublin.

Breathnach, N. (1994) 'John Marcus O'Sullivan Lecture, Towards a Coherent Philosophy of Education', *Irish Education Decision Maker* 8 (Spring): 4–10.

Carr, W. and Kemmis, S. (1986) *Becoming Critical, Education, Knowledge and Action Research*, London: Falmer.

Carter, D. and O'Neill, M. (eds) (1995) *International Perspectives on Educational Reform and Policy Implementation*, London: Falmer.

Clancy, P. (1995) *Access to College: Patterns of Continuity and Change*, Dublin: HEA.

Clancy, P., Drudy, S., Lynch, K. and O'Dowd, L. (eds) (1995) *Irish Society: Sociological Perspectives*, Dublin: IPA.

Commission of the European Communities (1989) *A Community of Twelve: Key Figures*, Brussels.

Connolly, M. (1994) 'The Report of the National Education Convention: Reflections of a Sympathetic Outsider', *Irish Education Decision Maker* 8 (Spring): 19–20.

Coolahan, J. (ed.) (1994) *Report of the National Education Convention*, Dublin: Government Publications.

—— (ed.) (1995) *Issues and Strategies in the Implementation of Education Policy*, Maynooth.

Crooks, T. and O'Dwyer, L. (ed.) (1990) *Education and Training in the European Community of the 1990s*, Proceedings of a Conference sponsored by the Department of Education and the Commission of the European Communities, Dublin: CDU.

Dale, R. (1989) *The State and Education Policy*, Milton Keynes: Open University Press.

European Commission (1995) *Towards the Learning Society*, White Paper on Education and Training, Teaching and Learning, Brussels.

Fianna Fail/Labour (1993) *Programme for a Partnership Government*, Dublin.

Garavan, T.N. (1995) 'Stakeholders and Strategic Human Resource Development', *The Journal of European Industrial Training* 19 (10): 11–16.

Gleeson, J. (1996) 'Senior Cycle Curriculum Policy: Rhetoric and Reality', *Issues in Education* 1 (1): 57–68, Dublin: ASTI.

Gleeson, J. and Granville, G. (1996) 'Curriculum Reform, Educational Planning and National Policy, The Case of the Leaving Certificate Applied', *Irish Education Studies*, ESAI.

Hannan, D. with Boyle, M. (1987) *Schooling Decisions: the Origins and Consequences of Selection and Streaming in Irish Post-Primary Schools*, Dublin: ESRI.

Hannan, D. *et al.* (1995) 'Early Leavers from Education and Training in Ireland, the Netherlands and the United Kingdom', *European Journal of Education* 30 (3): 325–46.

Humes, W.M. (1986) *The Leadership Class in Scottish Education*, Glasgow: John Donald.

IBEC (1993) Submission to the National Education Convention, National Archives, Dublin.

—— (1996) *Social Policy in a Competitive Economy*, Dublin.

Inter-Departmental Policy Committee on National Anti-Poverty Strategy (1995a) Consultation Paper on Institutional Mechanisms to support the NAPS, Dublin: Department of the Taoiseach.

—— (1995b) *Poverty, Social Exclusion and Inequality in Ireland, An Overview Statement*, Dublin: Department of the Taoiseach.

—— (1995c) *Summary of Submissions on the NAPS*, Dublin: Department of the Taoiseach.

Interim Curriculum and Examinations Board (1986) *Senior Cycle: Development and Direction*, Consultative Document, Dublin.

Ireland (1966) *Investment in Education: Report of the Survey Team*, Dublin: Stationery Office.

—— (1985) *Partners in Education*, Dublin: Stationery Office.

—— (1987) *Programme for National Recovery*, Dublin: Stationery Office.

—— (1991) *Programme for Social and Economic Progress*, Dublin: Stationery Office.

—— (1992a) *A Time for Change: Industrial Policy for the 1990s*, Report of the Industrial Policy Review Group, Dublin: Stationery Office.

—— (1992b) *Education for a Changing World*, Green Paper on Education, Dublin: Stationery Office.

—— (1994a) *Programme for Competitiveness and Work*, Dublin: Stationery Office.

—— (1994b) *Programme for National Development (1994–99)*, Dublin: Stationery Office.

—— (1995) *Charting our Education Future*, White Paper on Education, Dublin: Stationery Office.

—— (1996a) *Implementing the Agenda for Change*, Dublin: Stationery Office.

—— (1996b) *Partnership 2000 for Inclusion, Employment and Competitiveness*, Dublin: Stationery Office.

Irish Stenographers (1993) The National Convention, Days 1–9, Bray, County Wicklow.

Lynch, K. (1989) *The Hidden Curriculum – Reproduction in Education: An Appraisal*, London: Falmer.

—— (1992) 'Education and the Paid Labour Market', *Irish Education Studies*, Maynooth.

McCormack, T. (1992) 'Some General Issues in the Green Paper: a CMRS perspective', *Irish Education Decision Maker* 4 (Autumn): 26–9.

McGuinness, S. (1995) 'The Consultative Process in Educational Decision Making', unpublished paper read at ECER Conference, University of Bath.

Mulcahy, D. and O'Sullivan, D. (eds) (1989) *Irish Educational Policy, Process and Substance*, Dublin: Institute of Public Administration.

NESC (1986) *A Strategy for Development 1986–1990*, Dublin.

—— (1993) *Education and Training Policies for Economic and Social Development*, Dublin.

—— (1996) *Strategy into the 21$^{st}$ Century, Conclusions and Recommendations*, no. 98, Dublin.

O'Donnell, R. (1995) 'Decision Making in the 21st Century', *Political Agenda* 1: 29–36.

OECD (1991) *Review of National Policies for Education: Ireland*, Paris.

—— (1995) *Economic Surveys: Ireland*, Paris.

—— (1995) *Decision Making in 14 OECD Education Systems*, Paris.

O'Sullivan, D. (1992) 'Cultural Strangers and Educational Change: The OECD Report Investment in Education and Irish Educational Policy', *Journal of Education Policy* 7 (5): 445–69.

O'Toole, A. (1997)'Through Red Tinted Lenses', *Sunday Business Post*, 3 August: 26–7.

Roche, F. and Tansey, P. (1992) *Industrial Training in Ireland*, Dublin: Stationery Office.

Ryan, L. (1985) 'Unemployment: The Role of the Church', *The Furrow* 35 (1): 3–13.

Streeck, W. and Schmitter, P. (1985) 'Community, Market State and Associations? The Prospective Contribution of Interest Governance to Social Order', *European Sociological Review*, 1 (2): 119–38.

Sugrue, C. (1995) 'Critical Reflections on the Process of Charting our Education Future', unpublished paper read at ECER Conference, University of Bath.

Young, M. (1995) 'Post-Compulsory Education for a Learning Society', *Australian and New Zealand Journal of Vocational Education Research* 3 (1): 141ff.

# 4

# TRANSFORMATION AND REFORM OF VOCATIONAL EDUCATION AND TRAINING IN TAIWAN, REPUBLIC OF CHINA

*Dar-chin Rau*

## Introduction

The system of technological and vocational education has played a vital role in the process of Taiwan's economic development. During the 1950s, when the domestic industrial structure was still at a labour-intensive stage, most students who completed their elementary education entered junior high school, with only a few choosing to go to junior vocational high schools. Later, in the latter half of the 1960s, junior vocational high schools began to phase out while the number of senior vocational high schools increased in order to meet the manpower demand from the labour-intensive industries. Also in the latter half of the 1960s, the number of five-year junior colleges increased significantly and a new two-year junior college system was implemented for senior vocational school graduates. Both of the junior college systems were designed to train middle-level managerial staff and skilled workers. Also in the early 1960s the first institute of technology in Taiwan was established, bringing to the labour market through its graduates a source of professionally-trained managerial and technological personnel. At the same time 'vocational education' was renamed 'technological and vocational education'.

Over the past forty years, Taiwan has gradually changed from being a country, with an agrarian economy suffering from trade deficit, to a country with a robust industrial export-oriented economy which enjoys a high trade surplus. Now Taiwan is the thirteenth largest trading nation in the world with a per capita income of US$12,000, compared with less than US$200 in the early 1950s. Such a remarkable performance may be attributed primarily to the successful development of a vocational education and training system which produced professionals in sufficient numbers able to contribute to the rapid economic development of Taiwan.

The global economic environment has undergone significant changes in recent years and Taiwan has felt compelled to consider restructuring its provision for technological and vocational education. At present, the government is making great efforts to promote various important economic development initiatives such as the 'Economic Revitalisation Plan' and the 'Asia-Pacific Regional Operational Centre'. Efforts have also been made to seek membership in the GATT (General Agreement on Tariffs and Trades). Thus, because of these initiatives the timing is opportune for an adjustment to and, indeed, the transformation of technological and vocational education in Taiwan. The primary tasks in this reform will involve the design and implementation of a flexible educational system and the improvement of the quality of education provision. The reform should result in a better prepared and capable workforce.

## Vocational education

In Taiwan the Department of Technological and Vocational Education (DTVE), under the Ministry of Education (MOE), formulates rules and regulations for the implementation of technological and vocational education at all levels and its overall objective is to cultivate a skilled workforce to support the development of the country's economy. The DTVE has directed that senior vocational schools should provide students with appropriate knowledge, skills and work ethics to enable them to enter the job market. Junior colleges on the other hand are required to offer courses in applied sciences and practical technical skills. Beyond these junior and intermediate levels, institutes of technology were established to develop higher level manpower in the fields of technology, engineering and management (see Table 4.1).

The government has a very special part to play in implementing its education policy. According to the Constitution of the Republic of China (ROC), the central government should spend no less than 15 per cent of its annual budget in promoting education, science and culture, and for more than four decades this requirement has been met. The total education expenditure accounted for 10.45 per cent of government budget in 1952, rose to 13.37 per cent in 1972, and to 19.36 per cent in 1994.

There is a belief in Taiwan that the most important element in promoting education is to make it available to all people and in this regard, the length of compulsory education was extended from the original six years to nine years in 1968. The number of elementary schools and high schools has increased to move towards realising this aspiration. A tenth-grade compulsory vocational education system is now being planned for those graduates

Table 4.1 Number of technological and vocational schools in 1996

| Type of school | Institute of technology | | Junior college | | | Vocational high school | | High school with vocational training programs | | Total |
|---|---|---|---|---|---|---|---|---|---|---|
| | Public | Private | Public | Private | Total | Public | Private | Public | Private | |
| Arts | — | — | 1 | — | 1 | — | 2 | — | — | 2 |
| Agriculture | 1 | — | 1 | — | 1 | 6 | — | 1 | — | 6 |
| Agricultural and industrial | 2 | — | 1 | — | 2 | 18 | 7 | 6 | 3 | 19 |
| Industrial | 2 | — | 2 | 4 | 8 | 26 | 30 | 3 | 30 | 42 |
| Industrial and commerce | — | 1 | 3 | 30 | 36 | 4 | 3 | 6 | 11 | 67 |
| Commerce | — | — | 3 | 9 | 12 | 15 | 16 | — | — | 35 |
| Management | 1 | — | — | 1 | 1 | 7 | 13 | 1 | 1 | 23 |
| Nursing | — | — | 2 | 11 | 12 | 2 | 1 | 2 | — | 16 |
| Marine | — | — | — | 1 | 3 | 6 | 16 | — | — | 8 |
| Home economics | — | — | 2 | 1 | 1 | 10 | 16 | — | 16 | 44 |
| Physical education, (industrial and home) economics | — | — | — | — | 2 | — | 19 | — | 6 | 25 |
| Hotel management | — | — | 1 | — | 1 | — | — | — | — | — |
| Foreign languages | — | — | — | 1 | 1 | — | — | — | — | — |
| Military and police | — | — | 3 | — | 3 | — | — | — | — | — |
| Total | 6 | 1 | 19 | 58 | 84 | 94 | 107 | 19 | 67 | 287 |

Table 4.2 Taiwan's economic and social progress indices (1952–94)

| Year | 1952 | 1966 | 1987 | 1994 |
|---|---|---|---|---|
| Population (in thousands) | 8,128 | 12,993 | 19,673 | 21,126 |
| **Economic index** | | | | |
| Per capita income (US$) | 196 | 237 | 5,298 | 11,604 |
| Gross productivity of industry service | 67.8 | 77.5 | 94.7 | 96.4 |
| External trade (in US$ million) | 303 | 1,158 | 88,662 | 178,398 |
| Unemployment rate | 4.4 | 3.0 | 2.0 | 1.6 |
| **Social index** | | | | |
| Life expectancy | — | 65.18 (male) | 71.09 (male) | 71.86 (male) |
| | — | 69.74 (female) | 76.31 (female) | 77.72 (female) |
| Social insurance (in units of 10,000) | — | 156 (11.99) | 689 (34.95) | 1,261 (59.22) |
| **Educational index** | | | | |
| College level and above | 86 (1.4) | 263 (2.5) | 1,717 (9.8) | 2,495 (1.31) |
| Secondary education | 564 (8.8) | 1,676 (15.8) | 7,619 (43.3) | 9,252 (48.7) |
| Primary education | 2,774 (43.5) | 5,815 (54.8) | 6,607 (37.5) | 5,907 (31.1) |
| Other | 270 (4.2) | 402 (3.8) | 288 (1.6) | 203 (1.1) |
| Illiterate | 2,690 (42.1) | 2,458 (23.1) | 1,366 (7.8) | 1,130 (6.0) |

NB: Numbers are in thousands and for those over 6 years of age; numbers in brackets indicate percentage of total population.

| Year | 1952 | 1966 | 1987 | 1994 |
|---|---|---|---|---|
| **Living standard index** | | | | |
| Per capita living space (sq. ft) | — | 79.2 | 261.4 | 320.0 |
| Telephones (per 100 households) | — | — | 87.20 | 96.53 |
| TV sets (per 100 households) | — | — | 95.78 | 99.53 |
| Refrigerators (per 100 households) | — | — | 97.41 | 99.14 |
| Air conditioning (per 100 households) | — | — | 28.66 | 64.10 |
| Personal computers (per 100 households) | — | — | 3.55 | 15.29 |
| Cars (per 100 households) | — | — | 15.54 | 45.54 |
| Air travel (per 100 people) | 26 | 1,184 | 12,361 | 36,972 |

from junior high schools who do not intend to continue with their academic studies.

The data in Table 4.2 illustrates the success of the system in raising educational achievement in the period 1952 to 1994.

Apart from general education, Taiwan has continued to enhance the capacity of senior vocational schools to try to meet the increasing demands for skilled manpower. There were, for example, only 77 senior vocational schools back in 1950, compared with 206 in 1994 (see Table 4.1). During the same period, unit trade courses have been promoted in senior vocational schools to produce more skilled manpower and as a result, the ratio of students in senior vocational schools to those in general high schools increased from 4:6 to 7:3.

In recent years as referred to earlier, education strategies have been adjusted to reflect shifting trends in scientific and technological development and in the structure of industry and occupations from a craft base to a knowledge base. These have included, for example:

1 Slowing down the increase in the creation of senior vocational schools;
2 Encouraging the establishment of more comprehensive senior high schools and a six-year high school system;
3 Providing special classes in universities and increasing the number of institutes of technology to provide channels to senior vocational, five-year and two-year junior college graduates for pursuing higher education.

## Vocational training

A highly educated and motivated workforce has powered Taiwan's economic growth over the past forty years, and, consequently, labour rights have always been an important concern of the government. Legislative provision for workers' welfare is fully prescribed in the ROC Constitution as a fundamental part of the national policies. According to Article 153 of the Constitution, 'the state, in order to improve the livelihood of labourers and farmers and to improve their productive skill, should enact laws and carry out policies for their protection'. Under this constitutional provision, the legal framework accords workers equal opportunity to work and to pursue their rights.

The Council of Labour Affairs (CLA), the highest government office with responsibilities relating to the welfare and training of workers, maintains a comprehensive training system for upgrading the skills of workers. Although large enterprises have the capacity to train their own skilled workers, small and medium enterprises (SMEs), restrained by their lack of funds, equipment and trainers, often cannot provide satisfactory training programmes. To rectify this deficit the government steps in to promote and provide special courses that are necessary to meet the specific needs of SMEs.

In 1965, the government launched the first phase of a Manpower Development Plan and started to establish public training institutions which provided short-term vocational training courses. In 1966, with the assistance from the UNDP (United Nations Development Programme) and the ILO (International Labour Organisation), the National Service for Industry was established. This was followed by the establishment of more public training centres by both central and local governments. Currently, there are thirteen such centres and there are in addition hundreds of private training agencies through the country (see Figure 4.1).

In 1981, the Employment and Vocational Training Administration (EVTA) was established with a mandate to administer vocational training at the national level, provide employment services, and carry out skill testing. Further, Vocational Training Law was promulgated in 1983.

Taiwan in recent years has changed from a labour-intensive economy to one which emphasises technology, industrial automation and services. The

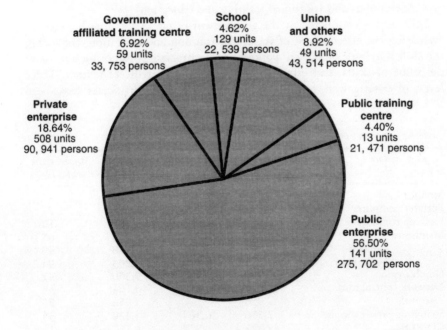

Total: 487, 920 persons

*Figure 4.1* Percentages of trainees by categories of training centre (1994)

*Source*: Technical Education and Vocational Research Centre at National Taiwan Normal University.

success of this transformation is attested by, for example, the data relating to Taiwan's computer-related products (see Table 4.3). In this regard, the strategies taken by the government have also been changed to:

1  strengthen and launch retraining programmes for workers;
2  provide job-transfer and second-expertise training;
3  strengthen training in the areas of computerisation, industrial automation, CNC, mechatronics and so on;
4  carry out more skill testing and improve the certification system;
5  provide training for manpower in service industry;
6  encourage industry to carry out training programmes; and
7  enhance management skill for administrative and managerial personnel.

The central government currently spends about NT$1 billion per year on vocational training, which accounts for 0.025 per cent of the total national budget.

In skill development, Taiwan has been promoting and conducting skill testing and skill competition and strenuous efforts have been made to provide technical and vocational training and education.

Skill testing conducted by the government began in 1974 with a view to evaluating the effectiveness of vocational training and education, enhancing the skill standards of skilled workers and technicians, promoting a sense of the value of skills, and establishing a vocational certificate system. Three levels of criteria were formulated for all trades and certificates have been

*Table 4.3* Taiwan's computer-related products (1995)

| Name of product | | | Domestic | Overseas | Total product | | Market share world-wide % |
|---|---|---|---|---|---|---|---|
| Monitor | | | 16,085 | 15,244 | 31,329 | | 57 |
| Portable computer | | | 2,592 | — | 2,592 | | 27 |
| Desktop computer | | | 4,167 | 400 | 4,567 | | 10 |
| Mainboard | | | 13,112 | 7,751 | 20,863 | | 65 |
| Scanner | Desktop | 2,481 | 1,278 | — | 2,481 | 1,278 | 64 | 49 |
| | Hand held | | 1,203 | — | | 1,203 | | 94 |
| Graphic card | | | 4,920 | 4,380 | 9,300 | | 32 |
| Network control card | | | 9,846 | 318 | 10,164 | | 38 |
| Terminal | | | 956 | — | 956 | | 27 |
| Switching power supply | | | 7,756 | 26,564 | 34,320 | | 35 |
| CD-ROM | | | 2,825 | 927 | 3,752 | | 11 |
| Video card | | | 1,663 | — | 1,663 | | 35 |
| Mouse | | | 31,087 | 9,817 | 40,904 | | 72 |
| Sound blaster card | | | 3,188 | 562 | 3,750 | | 22 |
| Keyboard | | | 4,589 | 28,190 | 32,779 | | 65 |

*Note*: Figures given in thousands

issued to everyone who has passed the test. By October 1995, trade testing had been introduced in 198 categories, and 719,655 certificates had been issued.

In addition to conducting national skill tests on an annual basis the government regularly holds special test sessions for enterprise employees and graduates from senior vocational schools and vocational training institutions.

In order to encourage young people's interest in learning trade skills, as well as drawing society's attention to skill development, a National Skill Competition has been held annually since 1968. Carefully selected competitors have also participated in International Vocational Training Competitions (International Youth Skill Olympics) since 1970 and many have had outstanding success.

There are three stages in the Taiwan process of skill development. The first is designed to develop a semi-skilled workforce, while the second aims to train multi-skilled workers and technicians. The development of technological manpower, as well as professionals needed in the industrial automation field and in service industry, are the main focus of the third stage. This stage also provides advanced technological training for those in employment. Taiwan, in its judgement of needs relating to future trends, is expanding the scope of the third stage and will continue to do so.

The skill testing system has won much support from industry and industry has given priority in employment, promotion and salary increases to those who have obtained certificates. Technicians from industry are invited to contribute to the formulation of skill testing regulations and to drafting test contents and of course this is status-enhancing. Workers have been eager to take skill tests. Currently more than 200,000 people take the tests each year, with 45 per cent of them passing and receiving certificates.

Many local businesses now offer on-the-job training courses. Every year, approximately 230,000 workers receive on-the-job training provided either by businesses or training institutes operating under government contracts. In 1992, the CLA assisted private enterprises in setting up a total of eighteen vocational training centres and these have subsequently provided training for nearly 720 job hunters, as well as on-the-job training for more than 6,500 workers. In addition, the CLA held ninety-six courses to train supervisors and technical personnel for public and private institutions, and over 22,000 workers successfully completed training in 1992. The CLA also offered vocational training to more than 2,700 foreign workers employed by investors based overseas.

A further prospect for the future of vocational school graduates is provided by government start-up loans to enable them to set up their own businesses. A maximum loan of US$20,000 is available at a low interest rate for five years.

## Stakeholders in education and training

The term 'stakeholder' is not commonly used in Taiwan. Instead, 'policy-maker' and 'general participant' are often used to refer to those who are involved in the decision-making processes of technological and vocational education and training. In this regard policy-makers include central government officers and university professors who serve as consultants to the government. General participants are usually employers' organisations, school teachers and school administrators. Major policy-makers of TVET are the Department of Technological and Vocational Education (DTVE), under the Ministry of Education (MOE), which is in charge of setting policy directions for vocational education, and the Employment and Vocational Training Administration (EVTA) under the Council of Labour Affairs (CLA), which formulates rules and regulations for vocational training and implements it through the various training institutions of Taiwan (see Figure 4.2).

The development of TVET and the decision-making processes associated with it in Taiwan can be divided into the three periods: 1950–79 (a centralisation period), 1980–90 (a consultation period) and 1990 onwards (a negotiation period).

### Centralisation period (1950–79)

During the period from 1950 to the end of the 1970s the government adopted a centralised mechanism for governing vocational education and training. It did so because only very limited and scarce resources could be allocated to education and these had to be directed to projects which could do most good to the economy. Policies and regulations formulated by the Ministry of Education (MOE) were submitted to the Executive Yuan (Authority), through the Council for Economic Planning and Development (CEPD), for approval. Under the centralised mechanism, the final decisions were made by the Executive Yuan, which would then inform the Legislative Yuan of any policies concerning vocational education and training. During this period, the ruling political party Kuomingtang also played a very important role in policy-making (see Figure 4.3). Industry and the country prospered under these arrangements and by the late 1970s pressure was mounting to loosen central controls and move to a devolved system.

### Consultation period (1980–90)

Between 1980 and 1990, the government began to take a democratic approach in formulating rules and regulations for vocational education and training. Views and opinions from local government were solicited and taken into consideration, and CEPD and MOE formed a partnership in drafting policies for final approval by the Executive Yuan. Earlier CEPD

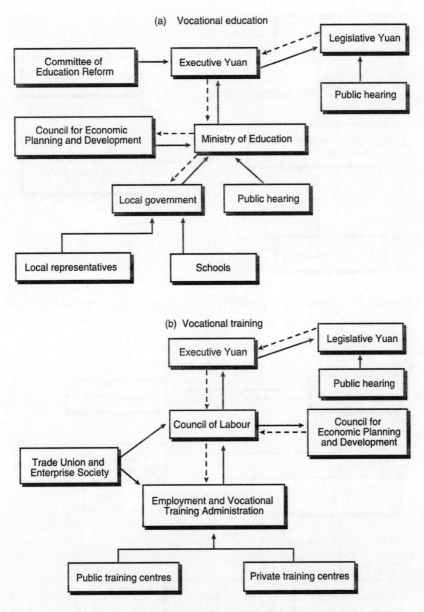

*Figure 4.2* The process of policy-making during the negotiation period (1990–)

*Source*: Technical Education and Vocational Research Centre at National Taiwan Normal University.

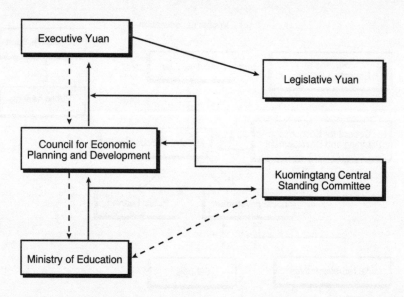

*Figure 4.3* The process of policy-making during the centralisation period (1950–79)

*Source*: Technical Education and Vocational Research Centre at National Taiwan Normal University.

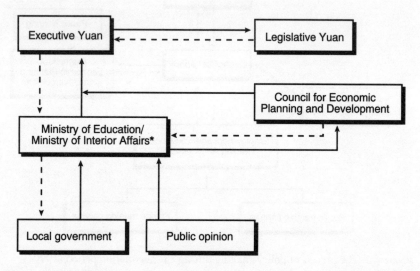

*Figure 4.4* The process of policy-making during the consultation period (1980–90)

*Source*: Technical Education and Vocational Research Centre at National Taiwan Normal University.

*Note*:
*       MOE – in charge of vocational education
        MOI – in charge of vocational training

was very much in control as central decision-maker. It was responsible for coordinating projects initiated by government departments and because of its overarching position it could ensure that duplication of effort and waste of manpower were limited. CEPD was also charged with constructing strategic plans for national developments and for devising blueprints to guide government departments in formulating their own particular long-term plans.

The Legislative Yuan fulfilled a different role in acting as a consulting body for the Executive Yuan on any decisions to be made (see Figure 4.4).

## Negotiation period (1990–)

In the 1990s, as Taiwan's society has become more diversified than ever, education policies have to be made through consultation among all levels of government. In these new circumstances, before MOE makes any decisions, views and information are sought from the bottom levels of the government. This process is aided by holding public hearings which help to ensure that the policies to be made are in accordance with the wishes of the general majority.

At the same time CEPD has become the consulting partner of MOE. The Executive Yuan examines the bills and regulations presented by MOE, makes necessary revisions, and submits them to the Legislative Yuan for approval. When a bill becomes law, MOE would cause it to be implemented at every level of government.

Media and public hearings referred to above are important tools in Taiwan for shaping public opinion and affecting the formulation of government rules and regulations. As the twenty-first century quickly approaches the roles of the media, local governments and their personnel will certainly become more influential than ever in deciding what policies are needed for future generations.

Parallel and separate arrangements apply for the formulation and implementation of policy to vocational training involving the bodies shown in Figure 4.2, in particular the Council of Labour and the Trade Union and Enterprise Society.

## Consensus and action

The government agencies responsible for TVET in Taiwan regularly hold cross-departmental meetings to achieve consensus and ensure policy consistency. In implementation, however, local governments often find it difficult to translate policies into actions. In the 'real world', there are some hidden obstacles to which the authorities of TVET often fail to pay attention. These include a strong public preference for normal high academic schools rather

81

than vocational schools, despite the efforts made by the MOE to improve the quality of vocational education and open more channels for further study to vocational school graduates. This traditional preference highlights the gap between any consensus achieved among policy-makers and the difficulties associated with implementation at local levels.

Another interesting example of difficulties associated with policy implementation relates to the MOE's proposal to elevate the status of vocational certificates. At present, people who hold vocational certificates are not accorded the recognition they deserve. In order to improve the situation, the MOE has proposed that public servants holding vocational certificates should be eligible for promotion and that any certificated person should be entitled to employment in government educational agencies. Although this proposal is the agreed view of the MOE, the Examination Yuan takes an opposite stance based upon the tenet that all public posts, according to the Constitution of the ROC, should be obtained through a national open examination process.

It is of paramount importance to note that where policy and implementation have proved to be inconsistent, there is an implication that the decision-making process did not take into consideration the extant situation of the 'real world'. To eliminate the gap described above between the praxis of the MOE and the Examination Yuan it is suggested that policy formulation should progress from the bottom up, and the implementation of policy from the top down. In addition, horizontal integration among policy-makers is important to facilitate better implementation of policy.

## Policies for the future

### *Strengthening labour administration*

The Council of Labour Affairs has introduced and continues to introduce measures consistent with its policies for the future, namely:

1 to guarantee the continuous growth of the economy;
2 to ensure that all workers, under adequate and reasonable protection of law and government, continue to participate actively in nation-building and make great contributions to Taiwan's economic and social progress;
3 to strengthen labour–management harmony and cooperation so that both sides can work together for a better future;
4 to enhance the quality of life of workers.

### *Training more professionals for industrial upgrading*

No system for policy formulation can be perfect, but whatever imperfections there might have been in past practice in the ROC the success of its policies has been confirmed by the growth of its economy. Nowadays the government is always willing to heed the expert in reaching conclusions about future directions for human resource development.

The great shifts and increasing liberalisation in international trade have prompted structural changes in Taiwan's economic development. This is best illustrated through shrinkage in traditional industries, growing output of hi-tech products and the growth in the service industry. To cope with such trends, the government launched the Economic Revitalisation Plan in 1993, aiming to advance industrial upgrading and develop Taiwan as a major Asia-Pacific Operational Centre.

Human resource development will become a primary concern of Taiwan's future education system. Emphasis will be given to the development of skilled professionals who will be able to contribute to domestic industries such as manufacturing, shipping, air transportation, telecommunications, finance and the media. In addition, a lifelong learning system and large scale distance education programmes will be launched to support on-the-job training and provide other learning opportunities for those in employment.

### Obtaining practical experience through cooperative education

Fruitful outcomes in vocational training and education can be achieved through two systems. The first is a 'simulation' system, in which practical training workshops in vocational schools are equipped with the same facilities as used in industry. The second is an 'on-the-job training' system in which work sites are also places for teaching.

Cooperative education where industry and education institutions make joint provision is a good example of on-the-job training. After more than four decades since its implementation in 1954, there is evidence that the provision of cooperative education in Taiwan needs to be more diverse and flexible so that students are able to get more benefit from it. Furthermore, industries should be encouraged to conduct cooperative education to provide regular training for employees to update their skills and technical knowledge. Three forms of cooperative education can be usefully employed, namely:

Students can be given one month to one year of training in enterprises
Schools can provide training for individual enterprises under contract
Schools can undertake research into training issues under contract from
    enterprises

### Providing quality education by shortening the resource gap between public and private schools

Private schools in Taiwan make a very significant contribution to the development of education, especially in the technological and vocational sectors (see Table 4.1). However, their support from government is much less than for public schools. With a view to redressing the imbalance in the distribution of resources and, as a result, enhancing the quality of education provided in private schools, the government proposes to increase their proportion of subsidy year by year, thereby encouraging fair competition between the public and private sectors. Indeed, this process has already started: for example, some private junior colleges individually receive funding in excess of US$1 million per year from MOE and this quantifies the disparity. The government also intends to make more scholarships available for students to attend private schools.

### Designing vocational education curriculum for the twenty-first century

The slogan 'think globally and act locally' advertises the emphasis for the vocational education curriculum for twenty-first century Taiwan. In this curriculum foreign language ability will be one of the key elements and another will be information technology.

Under the new legislation currently in force the curricula for higher vocational education are designed by the institutes themselves. Junior colleges on the other hand are allowed to specify and design 40 per cent of their curricula; the other 60 per cent is prescribed by the MOE. Via another initiative, teaching materials for senior vocational schools are being re-designed and enhanced.

### Conclusion

To effect appropriate safeguards for the future, the policy-makers in Taiwan should be aware that the TVET experience of other countries around the world may provide a valuable reference point, worthy of consideration in policy-making processes. In the United States, for example, community colleges are important resources for delivering education, offering opportunities for acquiring skills and training. These colleges not only give all people unlimited access to TVET but also offer an excellent resource for the life of the community. In Germany, students under the age of 18 receive one year of vocational training, including cooperative courses in enterprises of one- to two-days a week. This facilitates skill formation and raises the importance of TVET to the same level as academic programmes.

Vocational education and training now seems to be standing at a crossroads. It is taken as axiomatic in Taiwan that the development of vocational education and training in the next few years will affect the supply of skilled manpower for the future. In order to meet market demands, institutions at all levels will need to produce adequate numbers of professionals. This will be achieved by allowing more flexibility in vocational schools, strengthening cooperative education, closing the gap in esteem between public and private schools, and improving practical training. At the same time, curricula will be designed to meet the needs of all students so that their potential can be fully realised.

Changes already occurring in the expectations and aspirations of the people of Taiwan for a better quality of life and education demand an appropriate response. One possible way to deal with the situation is to implement a lifelong learning system that can be freely accessed by all the people. This would help them to adjust to changes and plan their ideal directions for the next century.

All of this will of course hinge upon the resolution of the conflict of praxis of the major policy-makers described earlier, preferably by introducing arrangements for a bottom-up dimension to policy formulation and by securing horizontal integration among policy-makers.

# 5

# DEVELOPMENTAL CORPORATISM AND THE PROCESS OF CHANGE IN VOCATIONAL EDUCATION AND TRAINING

## The Singaporean experience

*Johnny Sung*

Recent debates on national vocational education and training (VET) systems are increasingly focusing on two important issues. Firstly, it has been widely recognised that change may be an important feature of most successful VET systems. This is particularly the case for some newly industrialised economies where the speed and content of change are vital to the flexibility of their international competitiveness (Ng 1987). However, the relevant question concerns the way in which change is initiated, how change is supported, and how change is managed subsequently. Secondly, increasing recognition has been given to the linkage between economic, industrial and VET policies in the achievement of economic objectives (Ashton and Green 1996). For example, the creation of the Department for Education and Employment in England and Wales, and the Education and Industry Department in Scotland, reflects this particular concern. However, this recognition raises two further issues. On the one hand, attention is now increasingly focused upon the kinds of institutional set-up which may bring about better coordination among participants in the system; on the other hand, it is becoming obvious that consensus is a crucial condition for efficient and effective coordination to be achieved.

The above developments led to a rapid growth of two sets of literature in the attempt to explain how the different VET systems contribute towards economic growth. One set of literature concentrates on comparative analysis amongst the different VET systems in different parts of the world (Ryan

1991; Middleton, Ziderman and Adams 1993; Felstead *et al.* 1994; Godfrey 1997; World Bank 1991), and the other set focuses on the role of the state *vis-à-vis* economic growth (Wade 1990; Wallerstein 1979; Evans 1995; Rodan 1993; Amsden 1989; Okimoto 1989; Sung 1997; Castells 1992). The latter literature tends to conceptualise the ways in which societal elements are brought together to effect change.

We shall use the case of Singapore to argue that, in order to learn more about how some of the VET systems have been more effective in delivering change than others, it is important to identify the nature of state intervention. The VET system in Singapore has not been innovative, having inherited many elements from its colonial past. However, the system is capable of evolving with change due to a particular form of state developmental strategy which has a high degree of integration among different societal elements. By combining the two sets of literature – i.e. examining the Singaporean VET system from a comparative perspective and identifying the role of the state – we can see that the VET system alone is not the main source of effective change. The VET system has been effective only because of its strategic position *vis-à-vis* the role of the state.

This chapter will discuss the above issues in two main parts. The first part will highlight the VET structure in Singapore with specific emphasis on the integrated and changing nature of the VET system. The focus will also be on change and its relation to the different stages of economic growth. The second part will discuss the way in which changes in the VET system are part of the wider economic visions which determine industrial policy. This section will also explore the process of 'developmental corporatism' (Samuels 1987; Okimoto 1989) which generates 'national consensus' to support industrial policy and policy change. The discussion in this section will focus primarily on the state–capital–labour relationship.

The final argument of this chapter is that the institutional arrangement for the VET system, like other structural elements in Singapore, is merely a delivery system which pays close attention to economic performance and the nation's economic visions. The necessary national consensus, which is vital in initiating and supporting changes in the VET system, is derived from a more fundamental state–society process.

## The VET system in Singapore

The VET system in Singapore has a relatively short history. An initial structure was established when the National Industrial Training Council was set up in 1968 to facilitate technical education. This was a monumental period as Singapore formally abandoned the previous strategy of 'import substitution' to embrace industrialisation through 'export-oriented' manufacturing. The decision to abandon import substitution was an economic necessity since the entire economic strategy of Singapore prior to this period intended to form a common market with Malaysia, integrating Malaysia's rich natural resources with Singapore's trading capacity. The unexpected decision on the part of Malaysia to leave Singapore out of the union forced Singapore to look to an alternative economic strategy. The urgency of the new economic strategy was compounded by the impending withdrawal of the British naval base which had previously provided 16 per cent of overall employment and 20 per cent GDP for Singapore (Low *et al*. 1991).

The creation of the National Industrial Training Council was one of the important milestones to signal a major change in policy direction. As part of this change, the Council was vital in supporting two other major initiatives: first, the Economic Development Board (EDB), which was created in 1961 to coordinate internal industries for import substitution, becoming an active body in seeking overseas investment in Singapore; second, the setting up of Jurong Town Corporation (JTC) to oversee industrial development and management. The creation of the Council was therefore vital for the early industrialisation period which relied upon low value-added and export-oriented manufacturing. By 1969, in addition to the academic provision, technical and vocational education was firmly established.

Except for the recession years in 1973 and 1974 (the oil crisis), growth was achieved steadily throughout the period. By 1979, Singapore realised that low-cost competitive advantage could be threatened by emerging developing countries around the region. Singapore launched into the second phase of industrial restructuring – commonly known as the 'Second Industrialisation'. The Goh Report (Goh 1979) recommended a number of reforms within the educational system in order to deliver the manpower required for the following stage of economic development. The Vocational and Industrial Training Board (VITB) took over the running of all technical and vocational education through a series of technical institutes. This was an attempt to push technical and vocational training to meet Singapore's needs for higher value-added, higher technology and capital-intensive products.

Appendix 5.1 shows the structure of the VET system today. However, many of the features were achieved after the Goh Report reform in 1979. Appendix 5.1 shows some important features of the current system. To start with, the VET system is closely integrated with the general education system providing alternative routes for academic and vocational development. This reflects the desire to reduce 'wastage' and to maximise human resources. In addition, the system became more closely identified with economic needs (Low *et al*. 1993). The integrated framework is supported by 'streaming' within the school system.

In many respects, the Singaporean VET and general education systems show historic links with Britain. Students are studying towards the 'O' and 'A' level qualifications before higher education. However, the Singaporean system begins to differ from the British system in its heavy reliance on streaming and examination at every stage of education progression. The first streaming takes place after Primary 4, though at this stage the focus is on language ability.

The societal makeup of Singapore made it necessary to have different teaching media to cater for the different ethnic groups (Malay, Chinese and Indian). However, the necessity to master English in addition to the mother tongue imposed great constraints on the available learning time for other subjects.

After Primary 6, the Primary School Leaving Examination (PSLE) allocates students into the Normal ('N' route) and Express streams, in effect differentiating students between the academic and vocational routes. Since the exams are academically oriented, most of the achievers are following the academic route, leaving the lesser achievers to follow the vocational/technical stream. Students following the 'Normal route' are mostly destined to enter one of the Institute of Technical Education (ITE) courses. Some students who are successful in the S5N examination may be able to re-route back to the academic stream and subsequently sit for 'O' level exams. However, these students would have spent an extra year in the system, compared with those who have come through the 'express' route.

Another feature of the VET system, which is not shown in Appendix 5.1, is the parallel continuing/adult training system for worker upgrading. The system is managed by the Productivity and Standards Board (PSB) which oversees post-school vocational training and skills upgrading (also see Figure 5.2). Like the pre-employment system, there is a heavy emphasis on linking education to industrial needs. Most of the courses run by PSB are financed by a training levy called the 'Skill Development Fund' (SDF). The levy is currently set at 1 per cent of the total pay-roll for the low wage category (S$1,000 p.m.). Participation rates in PSB training courses are generally very high. The following are examples of some of the most noticeable training schemes:

1983    Basic Education for Skill Training (BEST)
1986    Modular Skills Training (MOST)
1987    Worker Improvement through Secondary Education (WISE)
1987    The Core Skills for Effectiveness and Change (COSEC)

There are two important features among these schemes. Firstly, the coverage of these schemes is extensive. In the case of BEST, by 1992, 78 per cent of the targeted workers (225,000) have been put through at least one module of BEST. Likewise, WISE has covered 42 per cent of the targeted 122,000 workers (ITE 1993). Secondly, these schemes form the main vehicle for continuing the up-skilling and re-skilling effort of the Singaporean industrial strategy.

To examine the relationship between skill training as discussed above and economic development needs, we need to look at the characteristics of the different stages of economic development. These training schemes did not emerge until the second phase of industrial development (1979–late 1980s). The reason being that during the first phase of economic development, the major concern was basic survival as a new nation. Singapore had to tackle high rates of unemployment, inherent racial instability and the lack of infrastructure and natural resources (Pang 1988).

Industrialisation through manufactured exports was identified as the most important 'survival' strategy. During this period, the skill debate was simply non-existent. The attention was to attract as much inward investment as possible to take advantage of the then largely unskilled immigrant labour force and the consumer boom in the West. Indeed, most of the industrial strategy during this period concerned the creation of an attractive industrial environment for foreign investment. As a result, most of the industrial policies concerned industrial conditions and the role of the trade unions. Arguably, these early economic constraints and associated survival issues had made lasting impacts on the psyche of the population. These factors also laid the foundation for the formation of 'developmental corporatism' (see pp. 91–8).

In the second phase, the basic industrial base had been established. Singapore, like Hong Kong, realised that the comparative advantage that they had enjoyed via low-cost labour could no longer be sustained. Countries such as Malaysia, the Philippines and Indonesia had an obvious advantage in labour costs, and were about to embark upon the same kind of industrial strategy that Singapore and Hong Kong once employed. The 1973–4 worldwide recession also led to trade protectionism in most of Singapore's overseas markets. It was recognised that there was an urgent need to upgrade the value content of industrial output. Therefore, BEST was set up in 1983 with the main purpose of providing basic education to a large section of the Singaporean immigrant workforce who had not completed primary education. In the late 1980s, three additional schemes emerged to further the skill building process.

For example, WISE was to take the general level of education of the workforce up to secondary schooling (i.e. 'O' level). MOST was to enhance the skills of semi-skilled workers. COSEC targeted the skill needs of service sector workers. The emergence of these training schemes was therefore by no means incidental but strategic. They support some of the most important stages of industrial diversification and high value-added policies of the economy. The imposition of the successive training schemes also meant that training was strategically preparing the Singaporean workforce for future economic needs.

The current expansion in the higher education sector is to concentrate on growth-potential industries, e.g. finance, information-/knowledge-based and high-skilled manufacturing. The creation of the New Apprenticeship Scheme (NAS) in 1990 which modelled the German 'dual system', reflects the belief that vocational training will have an important role to play in the latest efforts to create a high-skilled workforce.

The current developmental focus is specified in the 'Next Lap' document which sets a 'vision' that by 2030 Singapore will have achieved the standard of living enjoyed by the United States today (Ministry of Trade and Industry 1991).[1] The document contains details about the constraints and opportunities facing Singapore (with scenarios and responses specified). It also takes stock of the strengths and weaknesses of the Singapore economy. But most important of all, the document specifies the various aspects of development which are needed to take Singapore closer to the vision. The general strategy clearly relies on two major components: (1) the quality of manpower through education and training; (2) sustaining and enhancing the process of 'national teamwork'.[2]

## Developmental corporatism and the consensus process in Singapore

In an attempt to explain the phenomenal growth in South East Asia, a wealth of literature began to appear from the late 1970s. It can be roughly divided into three main groups. These are the neo-classical free market theory (Kuznets 1977; Rabushka 1979; Little 1979; Balassa 1981; World Bank 1993), the dependency and world system school (Wallerstein 1979; Henderson 1989) and the state/corporatism model (Wade 1990; Amsden 1989; Evans and Stephens 1988; Evans 1995). The neo-classical approach emphasises the critical role played by market forces and the facilitating role of the state. This approach also argues that it would be inefficient for the state to 'meddle' with market signals. Supporters of the neo-classical approach would point to the economic success of the Asian economies as being the consequence of high saving ratios, prudent macro-economic policy and a highly educated workforce (World Bank 1993). The major drawback of this approach is the fact that all governments have a series of objectives which ultimately lead them to intervene in the market. The Asian economies are no exception, and as in all cases, it is a matter of degree. After studying the development of the computer industries in different countries, Evans (1995) goes further to argue that contrasting interventionist and non-interventionist states is simply confusing the issue of development. The crucial question therefore is not whether states do or do not intervene, or by how much, but it is the way in which they intervene.

The dependency model is based upon a core–peripheral framework among competing nations. Within this model, it is possible for developing countries (the peripheral sector) to achieve economic progress. However, the developing countries are dictated by the dominant global system in which the developed countries (the core sector) will always maintain and control the flow of capital and the know-how, and therefore the pattern of the global skill formation process (Henderson 1989). The particular implication of this model for the Asian economies is that their skill formation systems (and therefore growth) would lag systematically behind the developed countries. The assumption is that state intervention, including that in the process of skill formation, will largely be 'reactive' to the flow of capital. The weakness of this approach is the lack of empirical evidence to support the hypothesis that the Asian newly industrialised countries have been hindered by the 'core' sector. The case of Singapore actually shows that the state and the capitalists have been able to accommodate each other's developmental goals. The result has shown that neither is the state a passive participant in the process of development, nor is development necessarily a 'zero-sum' game.

Developmental corporatism is a specific version of the general 'statist' approach. The general statist model assumes that the state is viewed as a dominant actor in the policy-making process. The 'developmental state' – a more restricted form of the statist approach which might have closer applicability in the early Asian growth experiences – is therefore a state that has the autonomy and capacity to set developmental vision, and this vision drives all the sub-systems and participants who are thus part of the wider process of economic and social change (Castells 1992). The concept of 'corporatism' has been used with several meanings. In the analysis of European industrial policy, 'corporatism' is essentially the basis for the tripartite industrial system where the state, capitalists and the labour unions are mutually represented (Katzenstein 1985).

However, when 'corporatism' was used to analyse the state–capitalist–labour relationship in the East Asian context (Pempel and Tsunekawa 1979), it was found that the European form of corporatism does not exist. Instead, a similar but distinct form of corporatism appeared to be prevalent in nearly all Asian economies – one that does not include labour. In most cases, 'corporatism' is practised with labour completely absent or labour being represented by a labour movement which is subordinate to the state, as in the case of Singapore. The policy-making process is therefore characterised by a continuing process of bilateral bargaining between the state and capitalists. This distinct sub-group of corporatism was later renamed 'developmental corporatism' (Sung 1997).

In his study of the energy industries in Japan, Samuels (1987) was probably one of the earliest attempts to apply developmental corporatism to the analysis of East Asian political culture. Samuels identifies two key characteristics within the state–business relationship. The first element is the 'reciprocity' of decisions which means that state and the business sector have equal access to that decision. The second element is 'consent' where a decision is made on the basis of 'interdependence' between the two actors. The combination of these two elements means that industrial policy is an outcome of continuing negotiation and compromise. Labour does not feature in the process (Sung 1997).

In the analysis of changes in the VET system in Singapore, the concept of developmental corporatism is very persuasive. Two particular characteristics form the basis of the applicability of the model:

1   In the attempt to attract overseas multinational companies to Singapore, the Singapore state, through the work of the Economic Development Board (EDB), has never been in a position to 'dominate' such overseas investors. There is no mechanism for compulsion. The Singapore state has had to 'compete' with other developing countries for such international investment. Therefore, the state–business relationship has always been based upon negotiation and cooperation. The emphasis is on the creation of mutual opportunities to meet the goals of the Singapore state as well as those of the MNCs (Schein 1996). The state–business relationship dominates the rest of the economy if one considers the fact that as early as the mid-1980s, MNC employment accounted for over 50 per cent of total employment, about 70 per cent of gross manufacturing output and 82 per cent of direct exports (Bello and Rosenfeld 1992);

2   Having persuaded overseas investors to come to Singapore, the Singapore state has to ensure that all factors of production in Singapore will deliver the desired results. It is here that labour is not automatically an element of the original decision-making process. It has to respond to the needs arising out of the plans made between the state and MNCs. This explains why labour activities (as organised by the National Trades Union Congress) are directed within the wider national economic strategies, and as such, why the VET system in Singapore is driven by external factors, such as MNCs' decisions to invest in Singapore, the pattern of international trade and the expected industrial developments relevant to Singapore.

Figure 5.1 shows that within the general corporatism framework, there is a mutual relationship amongst the three major actors. It also implies that these three actors are the only important factors that matter to the outcome. Developmental corporatism, however, shows the subordinate position of labour and other societal elements, including the VET system. The developmental corporatism half of the diagram also shows that not only is labour not part of the mutual decision-making system, other societal elements, e.g. the VET system, which are necessary to deliver an expected outcome, are also not part of decision-making process.

The applicability of developmental corporatism has immense implications for the development of the VET system. In most countries, changes in VET and general education are either the domain of the education department or jointly with the employment department. It is highly unusual to find that both VET and general education are closely influenced by decisions

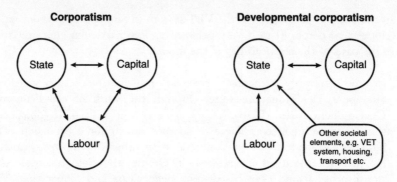

*Figure 5.1* The framework of general corporatism

made by the Ministry of Trade and Industry (MTI) via the Council for Professional and Technical Education (CPTE) (see Figure 5.2). In practice, the Economic Development Board (EDB) maintains a strong presence in all major trading cities/countries. The EDB's function is two-fold. On the one hand, the EDB serves as a 'one-stop' agency to bring investment into Singapore. On the other hand, the EDB provides constant data-gathering, feedback and analyses to MTI so that the Singapore government is always aware of changes and opportunities in the global trading situation *vis-à-vis* Singapore's developmental path (Low *et al*. 1993). Information of this kind has a major influence on the future development of the VET as well as general education systems.

Whilst taking into consideration the analysis coming from the EDB and the government's general development plan, the MTI transforms all the information into specific targets for the different components of the education and training system. However, it is the CPTE that coordinates the implementation of those specific targets. In other words, CPTE works as the major linkage between the education and training sector and those who are involved in the industrial policy section. On examining the composition of CPTE, one gets a clear view of how close the relationship between industrial strategy and educational changes is in Singapore (see Appendix 5.2). It is indicative that the Minister for MTI is also the Chairman of CPTE. It is also unusual to see representatives from NTUC and the National Wages Council. For the National Wages Council, its membership in CPTE reflects Singapore's acceptance of the close relationship between competitive wages and high inward investment on the one hand, and high wage and high value-added production on the other hand. The NTUC participation reflects the important emphasis of the role in education of the trade unions.

Within the framework of developmental corporatism, it would be

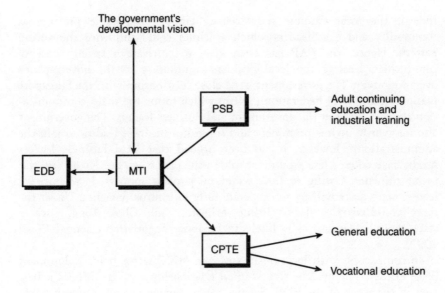

*Figure 5.2* The process of change in the VET system

misleading to talk about changes within the VET system as if the VET system had independent goals or a strategy of its own. The goals of the VET system are part of the wider national goals, driven by the national vision. Therefore, the presence of national objectives tends to form a clear and facilitating basis for national consensus amongst all those who participate. In fact, we argue that the consensus-building process is not about establishing a particular institutional framework so that effective communication can take place, on the assumption that this will generate consensus. Rather, consensus-building is about how effectively the process of (any) corporatism has been embedded into the state–capital–labour system.

In the following sections, we shall examine the nature of developmental corporatism in Singapore which forms the basis for national consensus and for change in the VET system. We shall examine the state–capital and state–labour relationships separately.

Much of Singapore's industrial infrastructure comes from western and Japanese multinationals and the local Chinese business community, though the government has assumed ownership of a significant number of industries and business, e.g. the airlines, shipyard, the Development Bank of Singapore, INTRACO (trading) and various substantial investments through Temasek Holdings (Vasil 1992). Foreign multinationals may come and go; it has long been recognised by the PAP that the local business community plays an important part within its development strategy.

Indeed, the local Chinese industrialists enjoy considerable prestige as community and clan leaders which at times could influence the voting pattern. Hence, the PAP has been keen to cultivate a strong sense of commitment among the local business community to the government's overall strategy. The government has a close relationship with the Singapore National Employers Federation (SNEF) which forms the main communication channel between the government and business leaders. The government also frequently invites prominent and successful business leaders to join the administration. However, it has been argued that local business leaders might have taken a less prominent role in the past when Lee Kuan Yew was prime minister. Owing to Lee's wide and popular support, local business leaders were quite willing to cooperate fully for mutual benefits. Under the more consultative style of Prime Minister Goh Chok Tong, such a state–capital relationship is likely to be more negotiation-oriented (Vasil 1992).

In comparison with local businesses, the MNC sector holds a dominant place in the economy. The state–capital relationship with the MNCs is best seen in the work of the EDB. Schein (1996) carried out an in-depth study about the EDB, its success and particularly its organisational culture in delivering the national goals. On interviewing MNCs on their experiences in dealing with the EDB, Schein found that the data from the different MNCs' executives, who have decided to invest in Singapore, were remarkably consistent. In the following extensive quote, Schein highlights a number of important features of developmental corporatism:

> The government was not only very aggressive but very professional in its recruitment of foreign capital. At the beginning they needed the foreign money and what was attractive to the investor was the sense that these people really wanted us. ... Access to them was always very easy – you could simply pick up the phone to your EDB contact and within 24 hours you could always get feedback of some sort. Their efficiency was impressive – they always worked in real time on the business clock, not on ... a government clock.
>
> ... when Mobil was involved in labour negotiations, the typical short-run philosophy in other parts of the world would be to just give each side a little of what they wanted. In contrast, Singapore always took a long-range point of view and asked the question, 'How can we resolve the issue in such a way that not only will everyone get what they want, but that productivity will go up?'
>
> Depending on the topic, there would usually be a short slide show indicating 'Here is where we are now' in terms of a certain set of issues. This would lead to a definition of a problem, or plan, or a set of questions followed by a set of proposals or ideas of what the Singaporeans felt they needed to do. Then they threw it open to the

industry executives with the question, 'What do you think?' ... There would then follow a very polite but open discussion relatively low on advocacy, but the industry executives would express their concerns ... the EDB people [would present] all the logic on their side as to why they had come up with a particular proposal. In this way the EDB would not only learn a great deal about what local executives thought, but it was also a very good way of co-opting those executives and getting them to think more about Singapore in a helpful way, leading ultimately toward regular dialogues.

(Schein 1996: 120–2)

The above example clearly demonstrates the two most important features of developmental corporatism: mutual access to the decision-making process between state and capital, and the acceptance of 'interdependence'. These features were also evident in Schein's other interviews with other MNCs, such as DuPont, Texas Instruments, Hewlett-Packard, Digital Equipment, Shell, Sony and so on.

The other link of developmental corporatism is the subordination of labour within what would otherwise be a tripartite framework. Right from the early days of Singapore's independent history, the PAP leadership saw it as fundamental to bring the labour movement in tune with the developmental goals of the state (Vasil 1992). In 1961, the PAP created the NTUC to rival a breakaway PAP 'leftist' faction which formed Barisan Socialis. Barisan Socialis was in opposition to the merging of Singapore and the Malaysian Federation. In the event, Singapore came out of the Federation, and the NTUC, with the support from the PAP, grew from strength to strength. Barisan Socialis became increasingly irrelevant, and was eventually replaced by the NTUC altogether. As a result, the state–labour corporatism discussion centres on the development and functioning of the NTUC only.

The previous discussion also suggests that labour does not feature in the developmental corporatist model as equal partner. Instead, labour forms a very important part of the socio-economic delivery system which is necessary to support the state–capital negotiation and decisions (as shown by Figure 5.1). The state represents labour within the state–capital decision-making process.

There are at least two areas in which we can identify the 'subordinate' relationship between the NTUC and the Singaporean state. Firstly, from its inception up until the 1970s, the NTUC was financially dependent on state funding (Gan 1977). It was supported by the Ministry of Labour and its Labour Research Unit (Leggett 1994). The unit provided PAP guidance to union activities, bargaining claims and strategies. Secondly, the practice of 'role rotation' has caused the distinction between state officials and the NTUC personnel to increasingly 'blur'. For example, in the early 1970s, members of parliament were also the executive officers of some of the larger affiliated unions, and at the same time, took up seven of the NTUC Central Committee seats (Deyo 1981). In recent years, the NTUC secretariat consists of one of the two deputy prime ministers as secretary-general, and three PAP MPs as deputy secretary-generals (Leggett 1994).

In addition to the internal composition of the NTUC, trade union activities are also governed by legal and institutional constraints. For example, through the years, successive pieces of legislation have removed militancy from the state–capital–labour relationship. One of the most important of these, the 1968 Industrial Relations Act, gave management full discretion in all matters concerning the personnel function within an organisation, e.g. recruitment, promotion, transfer, dismissal, allocation of duties, redundancy and so on. Pay bargaining is still the domain of the NTUC. However, such activities are guided by the Ministry of Labour, and any dispute will have to go through the Industrial Arbitration Court (IAC). The Court's ruling is final. As a result of such arrangements, the incidence of 'man-days lost' reduced drastically from their peaks in the 1950s (e.g. 946,000 in 1955), to a much reduced level in the 1960s (e.g. 11,000 in 1968), to a virtual absence of strikes since 1978.

The above sections have shown that effective developmental corporatism can lead to the establishment of a strong and cohesive internal structure amongst the three actors – the state, capital and labour. The issue of change in any of the sub-system elements, e.g. the VET and general education systems, and the consensus to support and effect such change, ought to be understood within the wider framework. In this respect, the Singaporean experience has shown that the debate about effective change in VET is unlikely to be useful if the focus is on comparative elements alone. It would be far more insightful if the relevant societal elements – social, political and economic – are also considered.

## Appendix 5.1

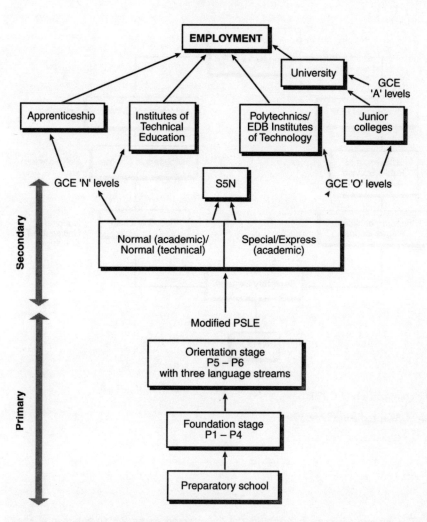

Reformed educational system (1991)

# Appendix 5.2

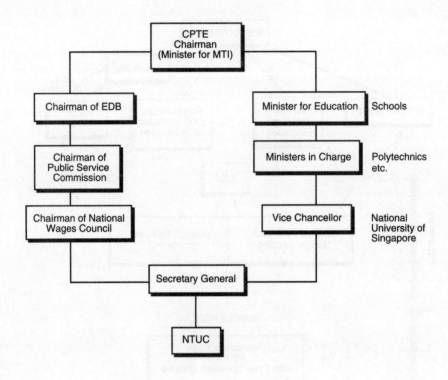

The composition of CPTE

*Source*: Adapted from Low 1991.

# Notes

1 The targets are staged: reaching the Swiss standard by 2010 and that of the United States between 2020–30.
2 The document states (p. 55) that national teamwork is to be achieved through: (1) cultivating and encouraging *personal values* which emphasise the importance of national teamwork; (2) practising the *consensus principle* without compromising the quality of the leadership process; (3) establishing *procedures and systems* which facilitate effective consensus-building, e.g. the use of high-level negotiation groups; (4) *discouraging class distinctions* which tend to polarise groups. [Italics are original emphases.]

# References

Amsden, A.H. (1989) *Asia's next giant: South Korea and late industrialisation*, New York: Oxford University Press.

Ashton, D. and Green, F. (1996) *Education, training and the global economy*, Cheltenham: Edward Elgar.

Ashton, D. and Sung, J. (1994) *The state, economic development and skill formation: a new Asian model?*, Working Paper Series No. 3, Leicester: Centre for Labour Market Studies, Leicester University.

Balassa, B. (1981) *The newly industrialising countries in the world economy*, New York: Pergamon.

Bello, W. and Rosenfeld, S. (1992) *Dragons in distress: Asia's miracle economies in crisis*, London: Penguin.

Castells, M. (1992) 'Four Asian tigers with a dragon head: A comparative analysis of the state, economy and society in the Asian Pacific Rim', in R. Appelbaum and J. Henderson *States and development in the Asian Pacific Rim*, California: Sage Publications.

Chan, Heng Chee (1976) *The dynamics of one party dominance*, Singapore: Singapore University Press.

Deyo, F. (1981) *Dependent development and industrial order: an Asian case study*, New York: Praeger Publishers.

Evans, P. (1995) *Embedded autonomy: state and industrial transformation*, Princeton: Princeton University Press.

Evans, P. and Stephens, J. (1988) 'Development and the world economy', in N. Smelser (ed.) *Handbook of Sociology*, Newbury Park: Sage Publications.

Felstead, A., Ashton, D., Green, F. and Sung, J. (1994) *International study of vocational education and training in the Federal Republic of Germany, Japan, Singapore and the United States*, Leicester: Centre for Labour Market Studies, Leicester University.

Gan, D. (1977) *The changing role of the National Trades Union Congress in national development*, Academic Exercise Paper, National University of Singapore: Department of Sociology.

Goh, Keng Swee and the Education Study Team (1979) Report on the Ministry of Education, February, Singapore: Ministry of Education.

Godfrey, M. (ed.) (1997) *Skill development for international competitiveness*, Cheltenham: Edward Elgar.

Henderson, J. (1989) *The globalisation of high technology production: society, space and semi-conductors in the restructuring of the modern world*, London: Sage Publications.

Institute of Technical Education, Singapore Government, Singapore (1993) *Annual Report*, Singapore: SNP Publishers.

Katzenstein, P. (1985) *Small states in world markets: industrial policy in Europe*, Ithaca, NY: Cornell University Press.

Kuznets, P.W. (1977) *Economic growth and structure in the Republic of Korea*, New Haven, CT: Yale University Press.

Lee Geok Boi (1995) *What if? Post-war choices in Singapore*, Singapore: Singapore Heritage Society.

Leggett, C. (1994) 'Singapore's industrial relations in the 1990s', in G. Rodan (ed.) *Singapore changes guard: social, political and economic directions in the 1990s*, Cheshire: Longman.

Little, I. (1979) 'An economic reconnaissance', in W. Galenson (ed.) *Economic growth and structural change in Taiwan*, Ithaca, NY: Cornell University Press.

Low, L. *et al.* (1993) 'Challenge and response: thirty years of the Economic Development Board', Singapore: Times Academic Press.

Low, L., Toh, Mun Heng and Soon, Teck Wong (1991) *Economics of education and manpower development: issues and policies in Singapore*, Singapore: McGraw-Hill.

Middleton, J., Ziderman, A. and Adams, A.V. (1993) *Skills for productivity: vocational education and training in developing countries*, New York: Oxford University Press.

Ministry of Trade and Industry (1991) *The strategic economic plan: towards a developed nation*, The Economic and Planning Committee, The Government of the Republic of Singapore, Singapore: SNP Publishers.

Ng, Sek-hong (1987) 'Training implications of technological change in manufacturing in New Industrial Economies: the Hong Kong case', a study prepared for the Training Policies Programme of the International Labour Office.

Okimoto, D.I. (1989) *Between MITI and the market: the Japanese Industrial Policy for High Technology*, Stanford, CA: Stanford University Press.

Pang, Eng Fong (ed.) (1988) *Labour market developments and structural change – The experience of ASEAN and Australia*, Singapore: Singaporean University Press.

Pempel, T.J. and Keiichi Tsunekawa (1979) 'Corporatism without labour?', in P. Schmitter *et al.* (eds) *Trends towards corporatism intermediation*, Beverly Hills, CA: Sage Publications.

Rabushka, A. (1979) *Hong Kong: a study in economic freedom*, Chicago, IL: University of Chicago Press.

Rodan, G. (1993) 'Preserving the one-party state in contemporary Singapore', in K. Hewison *et al. Southeast Asia in the 1990s: authoritarianism, democracy and capitalism*, Australia: Allen & Unwin.

Ryan, P. (1991) *International comparisons of vocational education and training for intermediate level skills*, London: Falmer Press.

Samuels, J. (1987) *The business of the Japanese State*, Ithaca, NY: Cornell University Press.

Schein, E. (1996) *Strategic pragmatism: the culture of Singapore's Economic Development Board*, Singapore: Toppan Company.

Sung, G.H. (1997) *The political economy of industrial policy in East Asia: the semiconductor industry in Taiwan and South Korea*, Cheltenham: Edward Elgar.

Vasil, Raj (1992) *Governing Singapore*, Singapore: Mandarin.

Wade, R. (1990) *Governing the market: economic theory and the role of government in East Asian industrialisation*, Princeton, NJ: Princeton University Press.

Wallerstein, I. (1979) *The capitalist world economy*, Cambridge: Cambridge University Press.

World Bank (1991) *Training on the threshold of the 1990s*, Education and Employment division, Population and Human Resource Department, Washington DC: World Bank.

World Bank (1993) *The East Asian miracle: economic growth and public policy*, New York: Oxford University Press.

# 6

# CHANGE AND CONSENSUS IN VOCATIONAL EDUCATION AND TRAINING

## The case of the German 'dual system'

*Willi Brand*

Germany has only very limited natural resources. Hardly any of them can be exploited profitably under conditions of worldwide competition. The main basis of its national wealth is therefore its manpower. The provision of skills through education and training, and the ingenuity and commitment of Germany's 82 million inhabitants are key factors for the wealth of the nation – and 'wealth' goes far beyond a purely economic notion. This paper is concerned with the question how the German 'dual system' deals on a policy level with changes in the world of work and what role consensus plays in that process.

## Selected key factors in the demand for change

Economic and technological changes have a deep impact on the VET system in Germany. Due to international competition, traditional German industrial strongholds in the machine-tool, electro-mechanics and electronics industries have come under heavy pressure and suffered slumps in sales. Employment shifts to service industries. Most of the following developments will be shared by many of the early industrialised countries:

- In 1997 alone there was a net loss of more than 460,000 jobs in Germany. The official unemployment figure has risen to over 4.5 million or 11.8 per cent of the workforce at the end of 1997 (9.9 per cent in West and 19.4 per cent in East Germany), the highest number since the Second World War. And there are many reasons to expect a lasting high level of long-term unemployment (see Table 6.1 and Figure 6.1).

- The volatility of market-demands has to be met by fast adaptation of production and distribution of goods and services.
- Changes in technology and – at least as important – in the organisation of work cause a high rate of obsolescence in the areas of work experience, knowledge, skills and attitudes.
- Growth in gross domestic product (GDP) has sunk steadily in recent years. At present optimistic forecasts expect a growth-rate of 2.7 per cent for 1998.
- Businesses have to cut costs; overheads – including training costs – have become a preferred target for reductions.

Under these rather bleak conditions the system of VET still keeps to its main traditional objectives: to provide a workforce with long-term employable skills and high motivation, and to help (young) people to develop realistic plans for their lives that meet their personal inclinations and capabilities with regard to their work as well as their social responsibilities.

What answers does the German VET system give to these challenges? How and where does consensual decision-making come in? And where are the major shortcomings in this process? This chapter is restricted to considering the policy-level and will not go into the details of curriculum-development and so on.

When we consider on which items consensus has to be reached in a change process, we find the following main decision areas in VET at the policy-level:

1  Objectives and content of VET
2  Responsibilities for the delivery of education and training
3  Financing
4  Control

*Table 6.1* Unemployment and GDP growth statistics (1992–7)

|  | 1992 | 1993 | 1994 | 1995 | 1996 | 1997 |
|---|---|---|---|---|---|---|
| Unemployed (%) | 8 | 8.9 | 9.6 | 9.4 | 10.3 | 11.4 |
| Growth of GDP (%) | 2 | −1.2 | 2.7 | 1.8 | 1.4 | 2.5 |

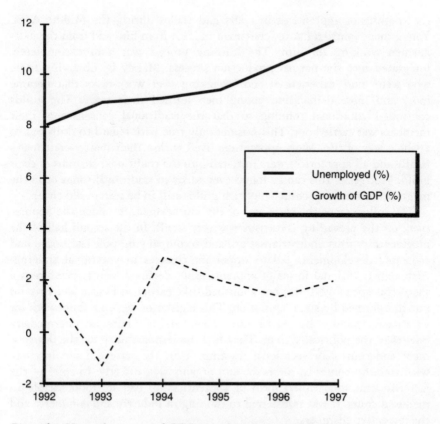

*Figure 6.1* Unemployment and GDP growth statistics (1992–7)

## The basic structure of VET in Germany

VET has had a long tradition in Germany and has brought about many different institutions, processes and procedures. I shall concentrate here on the so-called dual system for the following reasons:

- almost 70 per cent of an age-cohort pass through it
- it is a special system in the international context, which is only found in Germany, to a lesser extent in Austria and in the German-speaking cantons of Switzerland
- right now it is examining its foundations and its ability to change because it has come under pressure

(Other school-based forms of VET for adolescents and forms of higher-level VET for adults have a different structure and are not dealt with here.)

For several reasons consensus has played a major role in the dual system throughout its history. The most important root of this system goes back to the training of apprentices in crafts and trades during the Middle Ages. Young men[1] joined a master-craftsman to learn from him and from the journeymen working for him. The learning process was almost completely integrated into the normal production process. Mainly by observing those who were more experienced and by taking over work-tasks that became more and more demanding young men learned their trade. The guilds controlled vocational training so that the traditional consensus of their members was carried out. This was not only true with regard to skills but to a whole way of life. Many apprentices lived within their master-craftsman's family and all apprentices were initiated into the traditional customs of their guild. Vestiges of this can be found even today in traditional songs or in the magnificent medieval churches of rich guilds still to be seen in old cities.

The influence of the state and of the journeymen, let alone the apprentices, on the prevailing consensus was very small. In the second half of the nineteenth century industrialisation, and accompanying political, social and economic developments led to important changes in vocational training. Although traditional forms of apprenticeship declined, apprenticeship as a social concept of VET was not abolished (like earlier in France and Britain) but transformed by state legislation. This legislation set up a framework for vocational training by establishing chambers of crafts as intermediary powers in the political system. They had the responsibility for the development and control of vocational training. Thus the state did not interfere with training contents, methods, and organisation directly. In spite of the fact that this modernised form of apprenticeship had its roots visibly in medieval crafts, it was transferred to training in industry and commerce and the respective chambers.

These changes culminated in the gradual establishment of the dual system of VET one hundred years ago. Due to their difficult position in competition with emerging industries and other developments, the guilds had to accept that training in business should be supplemented by VET in special vocational schools (*Berufsschulen*) mostly financed by communes or the states of Germany. Gradually these schools were staffed with teachers who had a specialised training in theory and practice of a craft. Now decisions on VET depended not only on the consensus of the guilds but also on state administration and political bodies behind it.

Although pre-industrial crafts and trades were in the process of decline, the traditional concept of craftsmanship and the training for it did not vanish but lived on (Lange 1995: 102f.) and continued to influence the development of personal and social identities. There remained also a widespread consensus that it was the duty of businesses to take part in vocational training, including helping to meet the costs, and that this training had to lead to a status equal to the traditional journeyman: at the end of a three-year training period (approximately) each trainee had to take an examination which was overseen by the guild or the chamber of industry and commerce.

The purpose of the examination was to check that skills acquired were not only adapted to the needs of the business where the trainee was trained, but also to the expectations of the informed community of carpenters, bricklayers, shopkeepers and so on. The consensus about what a carpenter should be able to do had strong historical roots. And even the general public shared the consensus – although probably with some vagueness and some misconceptions. This consensual knowledge is useful when it comes to choosing a vocation for training or when setting up or replying to a job advertisement. It still plays an important role in the labour market and in negotiating wages and status today. VET had to accomplish more than imparting modules of qualifications which were thought to be useful for business. Indeed VET was expected to contribute to the development of strong, self-confident and self-sufficient personalities during a critical stage in life.

It was not by chance that the dual system underwent a major change in 1969 – a time when students demanded more democracy. The historical development had led to a proliferation of regulations, many of which had only regional or occupational validity. As a whole the system lacked transparency and democratic control. In a big effort the great coalition government of SPD (Social Democratic Party) and CDU (Christian Democratic Union) produced in 1969 the Vocational Training Act (*Berufsbildungsgesetz*). For the first time, it regulated in a quite consistent way, the framework of vocational training for the vast majority of occupations. The act was met with strong criticism from political parties, employers and trade unions – of course all pointing out different shortcomings. The fierce criticism made it obvious that only both great parties acting together could establish a consensus in parliament that was strong enough to pass the bill. Today, after nearly thirty years' experience of the Vocational Training Act it is safe to say that the act now meets with widespread agreement and thus describes a strong, if not unquestioned, consensus on the structure of VET. The act serves as a constitution for vocational training by providing the framework for more concrete regulations concerning the organisation of vocational training in businesses. At the centre of the act is the 'training-vocation' (*Ausbildungsberuf*); it has a recognised name, the training follows strict regulations and normally lasts for three years. Most of the training takes place within a business. Legislation did not discontinue the tradition of apprenticeship but left businesses with a strong role, especially on the operational level, and strengthened the position of trade unions, albeit under a more detailed framework of public control. For training in business, training-ordinances (*Ausbildungsordnung*) provide binding guidelines; on the basis of the training-ordinances, frame curricula are set up for vocational schools.

The duality of the dual system has many dimensions which affect the interests of stakeholders and make it necessary to find consensus on various questions. Figure 6.2 shows these dimensions.

Historically the foundations of this system lie in the apprenticeship of the guilds. About one hundred years ago the apprenticeship was supplemented by vocational education in schools. Business and school cooperate in a sandwich system – ideally each partner in step with the other.

### Vocational education and training in business establishments

The process of training is regulated by federal law. The student has to find a business which is willing to enter into a formal training contract with him. Both parties are obliged to choose a 'vocation' from a list of about 370 different accredited 'training-vocations'. The contract has to be approved by the relevant chamber of commerce or an equivalent body (e.g. chambers of the professions).

For each of these 'training-vocations' special training regulations have been set up by the federal government in cooperation with representatives of industry and labour. These regulations comprise obligatory elements of every training contract. They state:

- the name of the training-vocation
- the 'normal' duration of the training
- qualifications which have to be gained
- a schedule for when these qualifications have to be imparted within the company
- an outline of the demands in the final examination

About 70 per cent of the training time is spent in the company or in training centres under the responsibility of the business. Training within the company must be organised by a certified trainer, who is responsible for keeping the contract. He will be supported by employees who do most of the 'on the job' training. Only some of them will be certified trainers.

Training is controlled and the examination is organised and supervised by the individual chamber of commerce (or its equivalent). Representatives from industry and from labour conduct the examination in cooperation with vocational school teachers.

Companies spend about 30,000 to 50,000 DM on the training of an apprentice during the three years training time (including an allowance).

### Vocational education and training in *Berufsschulen* (vocational colleges)

Part-time school education is obligatory. It is regulated by the laws of the *Land* (State). Each *Land* sets up its own syllabi but these should be in compliance with the frame curriculum agreed upon by the 'Standing Conference of the Ministers of Education' from the sixteen States.

The main aims of the *Berufsschule* are:
- improve the general education of students
- supplement company training with a 'theory'-background
- take up and reflect work-experiences from companies
- provide knowledge and experience which go beyond the sometimes too-specialised training in the business
- prepare the students for their final examination

Students spend about 30 per cent of their training time either in a day-release or in a block-release system in the *Berufsschule*.

Teachers with university education are supported by a (decreasing) number of 'practice-teachers' (i.e. mainly master craftsmen) in workshops and labs. All teachers are civil servants.

*Berufsschulen* are supervised and fully financed by the governments of the States (mainly teachers' salaries) and municipalities (mainly buildings and equipment).

*Figure 6.2* The basic structure of the dual system

Reading the figure, one has to bear in mind that a training-ordinance is the central regulatory element on the side of in-company training whereas teaching in vocational colleges has to follow curricula which are developed individually in every *Land* (State). The latter have to comply with the respective frame curriculum worked out at federal level with regard to the training-ordinance. Training activities in businesses and in vocational colleges are coordinated and this has resulted in vocational qualifications that have nationwide recognition.

## Change in VET: the significance of training-ordinances

The dual nature of the VET system requires the coordination of many functions. This is especially true of the content of the education and training process and the coordination of business and vocational college (*Berufsschule*) elements. The key steering factor is here the training-ordinance (*Ausbildungsordnung*) which exists for every one of the 370 training-vocations. (In 1969 there were more than 800 such vocations; at present 97 per cent of all apprentices are trained in 260 vocations. Only 126 training-vocations are utilised in Hamburg.) Apart from a small number of exceptions (e.g. students with special needs) the Vocational Training Act of 1969 does not allow vocational training for young people outside these regulated training-vocations.

As one can guess from the number of just 370 training-vocations and an average duration of training of three years, individual training is very comprehensive (and expensive) in Germany. But this comprehensiveness is no safeguard against the need to change training both in content and in methods according to demands from the world of work and from society in general.

Changing demands have led to alterations in the qualification profiles of vocations, and even to the abolition of many outdated training-vocations or the creation of new ones. In 1974 a joint committee of the four main stakeholders (i.e. federal and state governments, employers' federations and trade unions) agreed to recognise a new training-vocation only if it fulfilled the following criteria among others (cf. BiBB 1993: 17):

1   sufficient long-term demand, not just based on the demand of individual (big) businesses;
2   geared to continuous vocational activity irrespective of age;
3   providing training with a broad-based vocational foundation;
4   duration of training between two and three years;
5   securing a basis for continuing training and occupational advancement;
6   development of the ability to take personal responsibility in applying knowledge and skills appropriately.

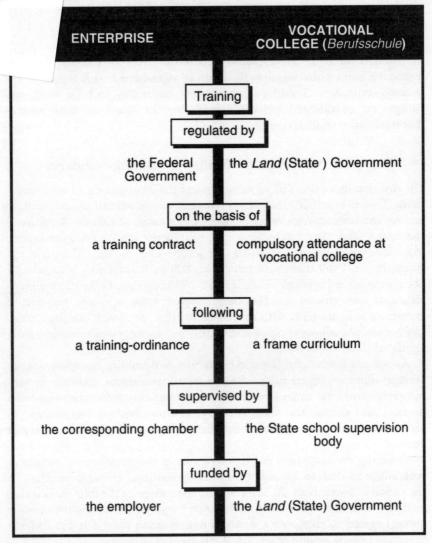

*Figure 6.3* The two partners in the dual system

*Source*: Adapted from BiBB 1993: 4.

Given these criteria, how does change come about in German VET? As the key steering-instrument for the actual training is the training-ordinance, it should reflect change in the world of work and at the same time anticipate it, albeit to a much lesser extent.

Each of the training-ordinances states:

- the name of the training-vocation
- the normal duration of the training
- qualifications awarded on completion of the training (vocational profile)
- a schedule of the training programme within the business setting
- an outline of the requirements of the examination at the end of the training

To a large extent the training-ordinance defines the respective training-vocation. Businesses are compelled by the Vocational Training Act to set up their individual training schedule according to the ordinance. It becomes an obligatory part of the training contract between the business and the trainee. On the side of the vocational college (*Berufsschule*), syllabi are geared to the ordinance so that learning processes in both environments can supplement and stimulate each other – at least that is the aim (see Figure 6.3).

## The role of stakeholders in the development of training-ordinances

Who is entitled to participate in the construction of training-ordinances? VET is considered to be of such high importance for the economic and social welfare of the society that the enactment of ordinances lies within the power of the Federal Government. The regulations are valid in the whole country across all the *Länder* (States).

Although the Federal Government is empowered to decide on all matters concerning training-ordinances, it takes a restrained position in the mechanism of the development process. Negotiations about training-ordinances are organised and facilitated by the Federal Institute for VET (*Bundesinstitut für Berufsbildung*, commonly abbreviated to BiBB). It is an organisation of the Federal Government. Its policies are decided by a governing board in which four 'benches' of stakeholders are represented in equal numbers:

1   employers' federations (e.g. Federation of German Industry, Federation of Crafts and Trades);
2   trade unions (e.g. Trades Union Congress, Metal Workers' Union);
3   Federal Government (representatives from a closely involved ministry, most often the Ministry of Economics, and the Federal Ministry of Education and Research);
4   governments of the sixteen *Länder* (States) that belong to the Federal Republic.
    (See Figure 6.4.)

Despite the fact that BiBB is funded completely by the Federal Government, the latter holds only 25 per cent of the votes in the governing board compared with 50 per cent which belong to the so-called 'social

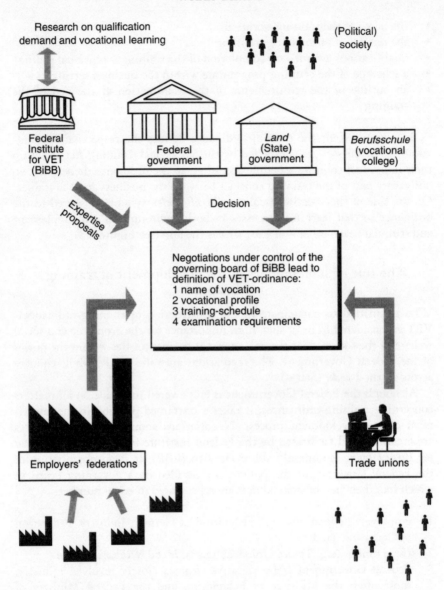

*Figure 6.4* The four stakeholders in VET policy-making

partners', i.e. trade unions and employers' federations. From the initiation of a research programme to the final proposal for a new training-ordinance all important decisions are taken by the governing board.

At the operational level BiBB maintains close links with all four benches of stakeholders during the development process so that their differing interests and views are continuously taken into consideration. The negotiations have undoubtedly a strong political dimension and the outcome is not free of political influence, but the *Bundesinstitut* has been very successful in rationalising the process by utilising research findings. Some of the research is conducted by BiBB itself but most of it is done by a wide range of independent research institutes engaged by BiBB after an invitation of tenders.

Politically more important for finding a consensus on a new training-ordinance is the fact that German trade unions are mainly organised according to branches of industry – a principle that was introduced by the British military government after the Second World War. To a considerable extent this organisation is congruent with the demarcations of training-vocations because most vocational training leads to employment in a particular branch of industry. Despite their existing conflicting general interests there is a relatively broad consensus of views on VET-needs, shared by trade unions and employers' federations. Although the federal government is legally authorised to enact the training-ordinance unilaterally, governments of all political parties have sought the consensus among other stakeholders, with special importance assigned to employers and unions.

## Phase structure of training-ordinance development

The process of the development of training-ordinances is divided into four phases (see Figure 6.5) according to agreements which were reached between 1972 and 1976. When any of the stakeholders (in practice generally the employers' federations or trade unions) proposes the development of a new ordinance, the governing board of BiBB decides whether it will take up the proposal. After the decision to proceed is taken, a four-phase process is started.

### *Phase 1: research and draft development*

Research on relevant qualification demands is initiated in order to produce evidence to decide on the criteria agreed upon by the four stakeholders (see Figure 6.5). Usually research comprises problem analyses for the development of working hypotheses, case studies and activity analyses in relevant occupational fields (BiBB 1993: 18f.). At the end of this phase a first draft of a training-ordinance will be presented to the ministry with the major interest.

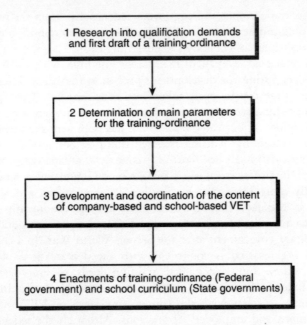

*Figure 6.5* Stages of the development of training-ordinances

*Example* Regulations for the training of office clerks were enacted in the year 1962. Unlike most other training-vocations, office clerks were and are trained in all branches of the economy. In 1989 about 74,000 people were in the course of three years of training – still conducted following the regulations from 1962. Considering the degree of change in information and communication systems, in work organisation and market relations, it became obvious that training regulations must have been partially outdated already by the mid-1970s. In 1983 BiBB started a research project to identify current qualification demands and elements of a new training-ordinance for office clerks. Subsequently a draft decision document was supplied to employers and labour representatives which was rejected by them in 1985. Only in 1987 did the so-called 'social partners' agree on basic principles for the restructuring of the apprenticeship. The long delay in agreement was not only due to major differences between employers and unions but also because of differing positions among employers themselves who represented, in this case, a range of business interests from big international enterprises to small workshops, since office clerks are employed in all sectors of the economy.

## Phase 2: determination of parameters

The second phase starts with the determination of the main parameters of the new training-ordinance by the ministry with the major interest during a conference with the stakeholders. The result is a 'project application'. After the governments of the sixteen *Länder* deliver their comments, BiBB is instructed to start work on the development of a training-ordinance that is built around the agreed parameters.

*Example* During a conference of all four stakeholders at the Federal Ministry of Economics on 24 May 1988, the following parameters were adopted (BiBB 1993: 20):

*Name of vocation*: Office organisation clerk [working title]
*Duration of training*: 3 years
*Vocational field category*: Business and administration [the 370 vocations are distributed over 14 fields according to similarities in content]
*Structure*: Apprenticeship without specialisation
*Catalogue of skills*
*Structure of timetable*: A new format of relating learning content to training periods is to be developed by a special commission

The parameters were integrated into a project application which then was adopted by both the Federal Government and the governments of the *Länder*. After consultations with the Federal Ministry of Education and Research, the Federal Ministry of Economics instructed BiBB on 27 May 1988 to start work on the development of the training-ordinance.

## Phase 3: development and coordination

Guidelines for training within companies and within vocational colleges (*Berufsschulen*) have to be coordinated in spite of the fact that political responsibility rests with the Federal Government and the State

115

Governments respectively. BiBB develops a draft of the training-ordinance in cooperation with training experts from employer and employee organisations. At the same time a work group of representatives from the ministries of education of the States drafts a frame curriculum. In mutual consultations both drafts are coordinated with respect to content and timing. After all parties involved agree, the governing board of BiBB is asked for its vote. A positive vote recommends the enactment of the training-ordinance.

---

*Example* In summer 1988, BiBB asked employer and employee organisations to each appoint seven experts to a working group. This exceptionally large number of experts is due to the fact that office clerks are employed in so many different sectors of the economy. The appointed experts represented four employer organisations and five unions. Until 1990 they had fourteen meetings with experts from BiBB and another two meetings with the working group for the frame curriculum.

Conflicts concerned mainly the following questions:

What will be the significance of shorthand skills?
How important are work-related skills in a foreign language (especially English)?
How should requirements of the practical examination be defined so that they can be well applied and at the same time do not restrict future developments?
In what format can content be related to training periods, so that flexibility and control in a broad range of different work organisations can be secured?

Mainly the representatives of small workshop industries demanded the training of shorthand skills. In a compromise this demand was not fulfilled in the training-ordinance for office clerks, but it was in the ordinance for office communication clerks which was developed at the same time. There the requirements were specified at such a low level that the skills cannot be applied effectively in practical situations but can only serve as basis for further training.

With regard to foreign language skills again the representatives of small businesses opposed the demands (brought forward mainly by union representatives but also by representatives of big industries) to introduce training in a foreign language. As these small businesses account for a high proportion of apprenticeships they had enough power to prevent foreign language training being declared compulsory.

Both other issues were resolved satisfactorily.

---

## Phase 4: enactment of the training-ordinance

After consultation with the Federal Ministry of Education and Research, the training-ordinance is enacted by the ministry which is mainly involved. The chambers of commerce (or equivalent chambers) are the main bodies which control its application in practical training. They organise and oversee the examinations at the end of the apprenticeships, give advice in all matters of VET, and make checks on the suitability of training staff, equipment and the range of work experience offered to apprentices in businesses.

BiBB has developed several instruments which enhance the understanding and support the acceptance of training-ordinances by those who are involved in training practice. Thus they have a very important function for the creation of a working consensus among those who are involved in VET as teachers, trainers or controllers of bodies like the chambers of commerce. These instruments are:

- explanatory annotations to the training-ordinance
- pilot projects to generate experience and knowledge for the implementation of a training-ordinance
- seminar concepts for the training of trainers and teachers
- teaching and learning materials

---

*Example*  On 2 October 1990, the training-ordinance and the frame curriculum were adopted by the coordinating committee of the Federal Government and the governments of the States.

By enactment through the Federal Ministry of Education and Research the training-ordinance for office clerks took effect on 1 August 1991.

The frame curriculum was adopted by the standing conference of the ministries of education of the sixteen States. The ministries modify the frame curriculum in most cases to make it applicable to the vocational colleges (*Berufsschulen*) in the State concerned.

117

In 1991 several pilot projects started to gain experience regarding the teaching and training for new objectives which were stipulated by the new training-ordinance. Furthermore these pilot projects produced teaching and learning media, a video to enhance the inventory of appropriate teaching methods, and seminars for members of examination boards to impart new assessment methods required by the training-ordinance (Brand 1994: 37ff.; Schmitt 1994: 11ff.).

## Deficiencies of the development of training-ordinances

A close look at the complex web of interests, power-mechanisms and procedures involved in the development of training-ordinances makes one wonder that results can be achieved at all (see Figure 6.6). Several checks and balances demand a consensual strategy. Although the Federal Government is entitled to enact a new ordinance without any consultations, it would not be wise to do so because the support of the State-run vocational colleges (*Berufsschulen*) would perhaps be lost, and in the case of severe conflicts no business would enter into a training contract with a young school-leaver. As the contract is a matter of private law, nobody can be forced to enter into one. All four stakeholders depend on each other in the pursuit of their objectives.

Several factors can be identified, which facilitate the difficult development process for new training-ordinances:

all stakeholders agreed on general procedures for the process (already in the early 1970s)

also in earlier times, consensus was achieved on fundamental issues of the formation of training-vocations (e.g. the criteria from 1974 mentioned on p. 109)

although BiBB is an agency of the Federal Government, it serves as respected mediator because of its recognised neutrality and expertise – supported by independent research and consultancy

the governing board of BiBB, with its four equally represented benches of stakeholders, is the central forum for the negotiation of consensus

Nonetheless revisions of training-ordinances take far too long at a time when the obsolescence rate of knowledge and skills has reached unprecedented heights. It is not acceptable that sometimes more than ten years go by from the first awareness of the need for change until the enactment of the new ordinance.

Other deficiencies seem to be inherent in consensual decision processes in general. Modern democracies depend heavily on decision-making processes

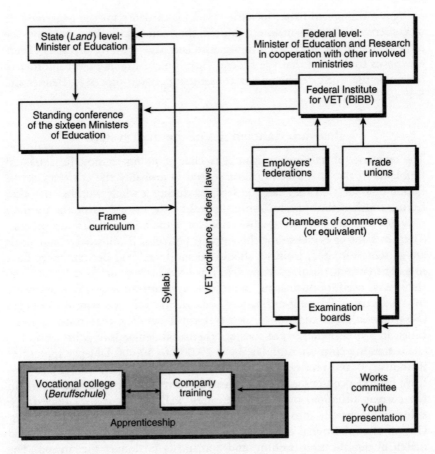

*Figure 6.6* Steering-relations in the dual system

which require consensus. The term 'consensus' has many connotations – for some of them we find ample evidence in the development of training-ordinances. According to Collins English Dictionary (1991 edn) 'consensus' means: 'general or widespread agreement'. This meaning is closely connected with claims for legitimacy. When we analyse the process through which consensus was reached, we find that a good deal of legitimacy is established by representational procedures once agreed on – and that does not necessarily result in high quality solutions. As in general politics there is a tendency to avoid differences in opinion and to occupy the middle ground. Thus consensus, 'while retaining a favourable sense of general agreement, has also acquired the unfavourable senses of bland or shabby evasion of necessary issues or arguments' (Williams 1976: 68). The bargaining about foreign language and shorthand training in the process described of developing a training-ordinance for office clerks is evidence for the negative side of consensual decision-making: limited shorthand skills help nobody; the same is true of the suggestion to organise language training privately. There are moves to demand that the Federal Government use its power in order to overcome the worst deficiencies of consensual decision-processes (Benner and Schmidt 1995: 3ff.).

## Relevant deficiencies of the dual system

The resistance of training-ordinances to change, points to more fundamental problems in the dual system. Most central is probably the criticism of the fiction of a vocation that can be exercised during a whole working life after having finished the apprenticeship. In reality, the critics insist, the training provides just an entrance qualification for a lifelong qualification process. There is a lot of evidence for this critical position. If knowledge and skills are so soon outdated, training should be shortened and become more flexible. The current training-ordinances leave too little room for adaptation to the special needs of businesses, interests of apprentices or new developments in industry. Training-ordinances, curricula of vocational colleges (*Berufsschulen*), and controlling bodies form a network that restricts flexibility, in contradiction to the constant rhetorical demands of politicians.

As training costs are high (at about 30,000 to 50,000 DM per apprentice in industry)[2] and profits low, many businesses opt out of training and thus leave behind a consensual practice that has been valid for a hundred years. In the current situation, businesses are often well-staffed or they hope to be able to buy cheaply into qualified personnel on the affluent labour market. One of the traditional strengths of the dual system, the relatively good match of qualification-training and demand is no longer guaranteed. The trades still offer training places because they are not so costly there. But the qualifications which are imparted there are often too limited and not well suited for future demands. Often the apprentices have to leave the business after their examination to make way for a new, cheaper apprentice. Of course this practice contradicts the fiction of a long-term vocation. For the first time in many decades it may well be that in the near future the percentage of unemployed trained youths will exceed the average number of unemployed over all age-groups.

The dual system has room for more flexibility but obviously it needs even more pressures from the environment on a process of substantial reform. It would be detrimental, however, to give up totally the idea that vocational education and training should contribute to the process of developing and stabilising personal and social identities – and instead only impart a collection of qualifications. The broader notion has been at the core of an emphatic and very effective consensus that had great influence on the German system of vocational education and training. It has to be seen

120

whether the forces of social consensus will be strong and creative enough to keep the essentials of this system alive under deteriorating economic conditions, new business policies, and globalised economic, cultural and social relations.

## Acknowledgements

I thank my colleague Professor Emeritus Hermann Lange for helpful comments on an earlier draft.

## Notes

1 In rare cases in medieval history girls could also enter apprenticeship.
2 Estimations of cost vary across a wide range dependent on (for example) training-vocation, branch of industry, accounting for overheads and so on. Interestingly, cost estimates have been drastically reduced during recent years. More than ten years ago trainers in businesses tried to improve their status by pointing at the high investment in training they were responsible for. After vigorous curbs on overheads, argumentation strategies were reversed and cost estimates reduced, mainly by emphasising the economic benefits which can be gained from productive work of apprentices and from their adaptation to work-procedures in the individual business.

## References

Arbeitsgruppe Bildungsbericht am Max-Planck-Institut für Bildungsforschung (1990) *Das Bildungswesen in der Bundesrepublik Deutschland*. Reinbek.

Benner, H. (1996) *Ordnung der staatlich anerkannten Ausbildungsberufe*, second enlarged edition. Bielefeld.

Benner, H. and Schmidt, H. (1995) 'Aktualität der Ausbildungsberufe und Effizienz des Neuordnungsverfahrens', *Berufsbildung in Wissenschaft und Praxis*, 24: 3–7.

Brand, W. (1994) 'Evaluation im Modellversuch "Neue Büroberufe" – Kontrolle oder Förderung?', in Pahl 1994: 37–50.

BiBB (1993) *Training-ordinances and the procedure for producing them*. Berlin and Bonn: Bundesinstitut für Berufliche Bildung.

Greinert, W. (1992) *The dual system of vocational training in the Federal Republic of Germany – structure and function*. Eschborn: GTZ.

Kutscha, G. (1994) *Berufsbildungspolitik und Berufsbildungsplanung. Kurseinheiten 1+2*. Fernuniversität Hagen.

Lange, H. (1995) 'Vocational education as an academic discipline and a matter of scientific research', in Helakorpi, S. (ed.) (1995) *Suomalais-saksalainen ammattikasvatusseminaari*. Hämeenlinna: 99–111.

Pahl, V. (1994) (ed.) *Neue Büroberufe – alte Ausbildung?*. Hamburg.

Schmitt, H. (1994) 'Der Modellversuch "Neue Büroberufe"', in Pahl 1994: 11–36.

Seyd, W. (1994) *Berufsbildung: Handelnd lernen – lernend handeln*. Hamburg.

—— (1997) 'Zielperspektiven beruflicher Bildung vor dem Hintergrund aktueller Entwicklungen auf dem Arbeitsmarkt', in Ellger-Rüttgardt, S. and Blumenthal, W. (eds) (1997) *Über die große Schwelle – Junge Menschen mit Behinderungen auf dem Weg von der Schule in Arbeit und Gesellschaft*. Ulm: 13–27.

Williams, R. (1976) *Keywords*. London: Fontana.

# 7

# PROCESS OWNERS AND STAKEHOLDERS IN VET REFORMS IN FINLAND

*Olli Räty*

## Historical perspectives

The history of Finnish vocational education and training in the twentieth century can be divided into three main periods.

First was a period prior to 1965 when the emphasis was on training as distinct from education. The training was geared to specific occupations and delivered in vocational institutes. These institutes were charged with the task of producing a skilled workforce to meet the needs of industry and commerce. Sectoral ministries, the Ministry of Industry and Commerce, the Ministry of Agriculture and Forestry, the Ministry of Transportation, and so on, lent support to the establishment and operation of the institutes.

A second distinctive period, from 1965 until 1987, was a time of centralisation and structural reform presided over by strong government. During the earlier part of this period, between 1965 and 1973, the administration of all vocational education became the responsibility of a new state agency, the National Board for Vocational Education, which was linked to the Ministry of Education. The NBVE had overarching responsibility for the content and structure of the curriculum, methods of instruction, evaluation, student enrolment and progression, and utilisation of resources, in all the vocational education institutes. Authority for the distribution of funding to the vocational education institutes was also vested in the NBVE, making it pre-eminent in status and power.

Later, from 1974 to 1987, still within the second historical period, was a time of great educational reform, in both vocational education and secondary school education. Driving these vocational reforms was the NBVE and it did so from an unrivalled position. The vocational impetus for these reforms was significant in providing support for a growing recognition of useful learning. These reforms will be discussed in detail later but suffice it for now that a system and structure for vocational education emerged which related quite specifically to all sectors of the economy and this structure formed an integral part of the overarching system of education.

The third and modern period from 1987 to date has been a time of unrest, a time of new ideas, debate and discussion about the future, and a time of cultural shifts.

While the reforms were taking place in secondary education, including the vocational reforms, vocational adult education, continuing or lifelong education was neglected. The need for reform of these latter components of the education system went unrecognised, or if it was recognised, it went unheeded. Now, however, it claimed attention and one important result has been the introduction of state aid for adult students. What has not yet taken place is an integration at an appropriate level of adult education with secondary vocational education.

Another force for change has been a wish for decentralisation and localisation of authority. Finland has been used to a top-down approach to planning but a desire for decentralisation will result in a shift in emphasis to bottom-up approaches, and of course this has brought with it some culture shock. The days of the big organisations seem to be numbered. A culture is emerging which sees partnerships and networking as offering better prospects for the future and it is against this background that questions about the way ahead are asked. What kind of vocational education and training system does Finland want and how open and flexible should it be? What would be the roles of the institutions and their teachers? How should regional government relate to the institutions or indeed should there be any kind of formal relationship at all or should the institutions be independent?

There is a weariness hovering about in vocational education: teachers and educationalists are tired after the great reforms of vocational education and they are unwilling to take on new initiatives. However, some projects have been forced upon the weary. Two are particularly important and they are large in resource terms. One relates to establishing new polytechnic type institutes (like the German *Fachhochschule*) and the other relates to local integration of vocational education and general secondary education. It is proposed to create twenty-two experimental polytechnics by merging colleges or, in the case of very large colleges, by re-designating them. Following a successful piloting exercise nine permanent polytechnics were founded in 1996. On the integration initiative some limited progress has been made. Schools and institutes may collaborate so that students may accumulate credit for both general and vocational education, but more of this later.

## The 'great reform' of vocational education of 1970s and 1980s

The process of reform began with a reorganisation of the national administrative framework for vocational education and the establishment of the

National Board of Vocational Education (NBVE) and proceeded thereafter by delegating tasks and responsibilities to a series of committees, each committee having a clearly defined remit (see Figure 7.1).

As a second step, three national committees were set up to generate basic ideas and principles which could shape the reform and to promote public discussion. The committees sat until 1974 at which point the government decided upon the principles which would underpin the reform process. Work then proceeded apace.

Development committees – fourteen in all, covering all sectors of the economy – were set up with a working life of three years until 1977, each with a mandate to prescribe a structure for vocational education provision for its sector. Once the structures had been approved at central government level, the committees were charged with a new task of formulating curricula for all vocational qualifications in their respective sectors.

Other major committees were formed which operated in parallel with the vocational committees. Of prime importance was the committee which led the whole reform process for the totality of education provision. A second committee had the task of preparing curricula for general secondary education and a third committee had to look at ways of integrating vocational education into primary education.

The work of all of the committees culminated in the Act of the Development of Education passed in 1978. This Act authorised the development and introduction of a new educational structure with pilot projects to begin immediately. Also included in the Act were enabling modifications to existing legislation to facilitate the introduction of the new curricula.

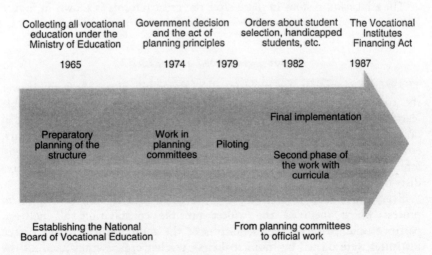

*Figure 7.1* Implementation of the VET reform

OLLI RÄTY

While the pilot schemes were running, further work was undertaken to finalise the curricula for each sector and to arrange for its delivery throughout the country. This also included plans for student enrolment and initiatives were introduced for a nationwide system for student selection and for the integration of handicapped students into normal state education provision. Preliminary work was concluded by 1982 at which time new curricula began to be adopted sector by sector and continued until the process was completed in 1988. This phase of the reforms saw: (1) a new structure/system of vocational education together with new curricula; (2) a nationwide computer-based student selection system; and (3) state-wide and regional planning of student enrolments for all levels of vocational courses. It also saw the introduction of a new guidance system, the construction of buildings for new education institutes or to enlarge old ones, and the publication of new learning materials.

It was disappointing that while there was undoubted success in the reforms to vocational education and training, the hoped for integration of vocational education into the general secondary school system did not come to pass. Integration into the primary school was more successful. The comprehensive school curricula were modified so that every student who passed the comprehensive school examination was able to continue either in general secondary education (high school) or in vocational education.

Three acts were passed in 1987 which finally established a new framework for vocational education and training. One act related to vocational education institutes, a second act was concerned with the finance of vocational education, and a third act was devoted to support for students, i.e. an act of student social subsidising.

The education system in place after the great reforms is shown in Figure 7.2.

## What was learned and gained?

The reform process as described involved thousands of people from all over the country. It was very time-consuming but it provided an invaluable learning experience for everyone who participated. Before the reforms began no one had a clearly defined responsibility for vocational education affairs, either at national or local level, and one of the first reform tasks was therefore to establish an appropriate administrative system with an effective distribution of powers backed up by the necessary protocols.

Every conceivable interested party was taken into account in the reform process which included the widest possible consultation: all political parties, social partners, representatives of the municipalities (most of the institutes were owned by municipalities), teacher organisations, and all the people working in institutes or in state and regional agencies had their say.

126

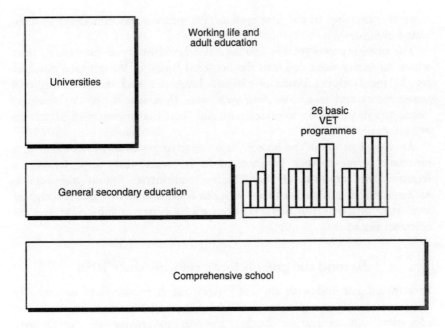

*Figure 7.2* Structure of education after VET reform

As well as the action being taken at national level, much work was carried out by task groups and cooperative councils acting at institute and regional levels.

Specialised sectoral work was divided among fourteen committees laying down the parameters for courses in all vocational areas. Plans were drawn up for about 250 specialised degrees across twenty-five basic sectors (increased later to twenty-six). About 3,500 different subjects were accommodated in this exercise and much credit for the developmental work goes to experts not only from the institutes but also from industry and commerce who made important contributions.

## The multilevel planning as a precursor to decentralisation

It is clear from what has been described so far that the government was anxious to get all interests caught up in the reform process. It could then act additionally as a familiarisation process where vocational education was concerned. The knowledge and understanding of vocational education provision which would flow from taking part in the consultations would be helpful when decentralisation was introduced. Another intended outcome of the participation of all interested parties, stakeholders, or whatever, was a sense of ownership in the new system. The process was multilevel as illustrated in Figure 7.3.

The planning process was initiated by the Ministry of Education, from where directives went down to the National Board of Vocational Education and to the National Board of General Education and thence to regional governments and institutes. Proposals were then sent up to the National Board where proposals were collated and final documents drafted for the Ministry of Education.

At critical points in the process, legislation or government decisions were necessary before further progress could be sanctioned. Such legislation required the approval of the 'leading committee' whose membership included politicians with a major locus in education affairs, and the highest level state officers (civil servants) from the Ministry of Education and the National Boards.

## Beyond the great reform: reforms since 1988

Reform did not end with the 1987 Acts: much remained to be done. In 1991 a major step was taken towards enhancing the status of vocational education and generating further impetus for parity of esteem with 'academic' education by the merger of the National Board of Education and the National Board of Vocational Education. At the same time national industry-education councils were set up for every branch of vocational

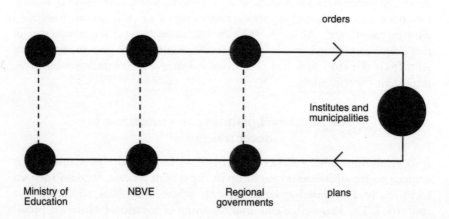

*Figure* 7.3 The multilevel planning process

education, and these councils have had a key role in decision-making in connection with the reforms of the 1990s.

In 1987–8 the government, after detailed consultation, approved a set of principles for the organisation of adult education and its finance, and these were later embodied in the Social Benefit Act. New legislation followed which made it possible for adults to sit vocational qualifications examinations without undertaking lengthy formal courses of instruction in education establishments. These changes in provision were generally welcomed since they offer new flexible access to education.

Perhaps the most significant development of the post-1987 period was the government memorandum of the future structure for the whole education system, shown diagrammatically in Figure 7.4. This was an ambitious proposal which would see the establishment of a dual system for post-school higher education with the universities and art academies on the one hand, and polytechnics on the other. Also encapsulated in the proposal was substantial provision for adult education which would accommodate about 35,000 students per year through the flexible arrangement referred to above, and a further 15,000 per year going into higher education. Senior secondary schools and vocational education establishments would be expanded to accommodate 10,000 to 15,000 adults per year (see Figure 7.4).

While the two projects relating to the formation of the polytechnics and the integration of vocational education and secondary education were reviewed there was a lull in activity. However, it did not last for long.

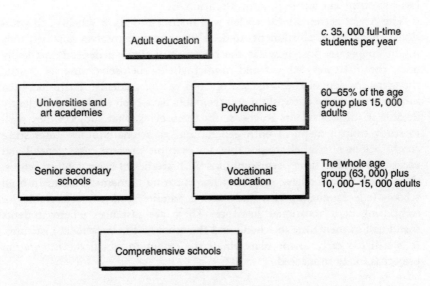

*Figure* 7.4 Government proposal for the future structure of education

Approval was given for the continuation of both projects until 1999, at which time a final decision would be taken about the structure of the education system.

Where the polytechnics were concerned it was decided that their programmes should be geared to the needs of practically oriented education, i.e. education geared to industry, commerce and the professions.

The new polytechnics have been welcomed with enthusiasm, but not without opposition from some university quarters. A new form of higher education, particularly one open to those who have completed secondary education in the VET sector and not passed the secondary matriculation examination or the university entrance examinations, was unlikely to find favour with the universities. It had appeal however for families from all classes because of the opportunities it presented for high-level vocational education. The new route from the comprehensive school via vocational education to higher education was a stimulus for fresh ideas about the scope and purpose of education and added an option for 'practical education' within higher education, particularly for professional education, which had been absent hitherto. Had there been more involvement of university staff in the development of VET perhaps there would have been less dissent. Polytechnics and polytechnic education are now firmly located alongside university provision as the major second component in the higher education framework.

Progress with the integration of vocational education and general education, the second major project, has been less spectacular. This project has been largely overshadowed by the polytechnic project and has been much less successful in claiming public attention.

The Act of Secondary Education was amended to allow schools and vocational education establishments to decide amongst themselves how best they might cooperate. Just how far the reform will succeed depends markedly upon the institutes, schools and municipalities themselves and, of course, the attractiveness of the proposed options to the students. There has been some success where curriculum arrangements have been rendered sufficiently flexible to allow students to choose for themselves what subjects they wish to study from a menu of both general and vocational studies. Interesting combinations of studies are possible, for example in some cases general and vocational studies have been combined with studies of sport, golf or tennis. Other contributions have seen students pursuing academic studies in high schools (e.g. languages) and undertaking parallel studies in electronics or computing at a vocational institute. There are instances where students spend half of their time in schools and the other half in vocational institutes. It is still too early to speculate about the extent to which the integration project is likely to succeed.

## Who were the process owners and the stakeholders in the great reform?

Having looked at the nature of reforms of Finnish education since 1965 it is time to take a closer look at the people and agents who were associated with them, i.e. the stakeholders and interested parties. There were seven important groups – politicians, social partners, the association of municipalities, publishing houses and writers, principals and teachers, the media, and lastly the old high status group at the head of general secondary education – who had different important loci in the reform processes, and each will be examined in turn.

Politics and government in Finland invariably involve a coalition of political parties. In the present parliament there are representatives of twelve parties but in the 1970s there were only seven or eight. Since the Second World War the Social Democrats have always been the party with the highest proportion of representatives but this amounts to as little as 25 per cent of the total. The two other big parties are the Conservatives and the Centre Party (Agrarian Party) both of which usually have about 20 per cent of the representatives. Usually two of the big parties will form a coalition.

When the great reform began in the early 1970s there was a coalition of four parties, the Social Democrats, the Centre Party, the Communist Party and the Swedish Party, with the Conservatives leading the opposition. Most of the state officers had leanings towards either the Social Democrats or the Conservatives, and by this time officers who were adherents to the Centre Party began to appear in ministries other than the Ministry of Agriculture and Forestry. The Centre Party was and still is a major force in rural areas and therefore exerts control over many of the vocational institutes owned by the municipalities.

Under the early 1970s coalition arrangements, the membership of all state/government committees had to reflect the composition of the coalition, i.e. each of the big parties, the Social Democrats and the Centre Party, and one member each from the Communist Party and the Swedish Party. The secretariat of the committees was also balanced between affiliates of the two big parties.

At this time active involvement in politics was time-consuming and expensive but it was, and is, very important that influential and knowledgeable people are able to participate. Politicians were a very important group of stakeholders in the reform process. Some were members of the lead committee and others contributed to the work of the sector committees where they exercised not only political judgement but professional judgement. The chairman of the planning committee for the sector of health education, for example, was both a doctor and a member of the Social Democrats' representation in parliament.

Social partners comprising employers' and employees' unions were a second group of stakeholders. This group was strongly represented on all important committees. Its main interest was in securing a kind of education provision which could safeguard employment prospects for the future. Employers sought the kind of education and training provision which would provide a skilled and capable workforce, and employees sought provision which would enhance employability and capability in the labour market and as citizens. Social partners were also encouraged to take part in schools' councils so that they could be party to decision-making at local level.

Unfortunately the employers' organisation took a blinkered view. It was unwilling to support any alternative to a dual system based on German lines for apprentice training and thus was at odds with the school-based system espoused by the education lobby. But even if the employers had got their way and a dual system had been introduced they would have been reluctant, even unwilling, to accept a share of the costs. In general, employers saw the reforms as being driven by left-wing politicians and civil servants. Employees took a different view, very much in line with the educators: they wanted longer and broader vocational education courses which could lead on from secondary education to higher and adult education.

A third major stakeholder was the Association of Municipalities whose prime objective was to ensure that whatever system was to be introduced there should be an equitable attribution of costs to both the state and the municipalities.

Publishing houses and writers constituted a fourth group of stakeholders of a different kind and with different interests. Any major curriculum reforms would be likely to require the production of a new range of curriculum support materials and this would present opportunities to publishers and writers.

No curriculum reform can succeed without the support of principals and teachers, whether it be willing support or reluctant support, and these groups were therefore among the most influential stakeholders in the reform process. Their role in the process was limited, being restricted to matters of implementation in their own establishments including local enrolment of students. Curricula were drafted by 'experts' working for the sectoral planning committees. This meant that curricula and supporting teaching materials were produced centrally and distributed to those at the delivery end.

At the conclusion of the great reform in 1987 this was changed with new legislation whereby the Ministry of Education provided curriculum guidelines for each sector and thereafter it was up to principals and teachers to prepare the curricula to be delivered in their own institutions. This meant local development of teaching processes and this required preparation or acquisition of resource materials.

Traditionally the media showed little interest in vocational education. In the main, newspapers, radio and television were peopled by the affluent and their interests lay more in high status education, in universities or other higher education institutes i.e. health education institutes and a few technical colleges which offer high-level courses. These interests reflected employment prospects and in particular the routes into the professions. And this was the case in Finland until the collapse of the Soviet Union which had caused such a downturn in the Finnish economy with a concomitant abrupt rise in unemployment. Exports from Finland dropped by 20 per cent and unemployment rose from 3 per cent to 19 per cent (in 1996 unemployment is still running at about 17 per cent). Unemployment struck right across the workforce, not only manual workers, skilled, semi-skilled and unskilled, but many professionals were also affected. Job expectations changed and interest grew in all kinds of education which related to occupations because such forms of education brought with them some prospect of a job. Vocational education and training was seen as a tool with which to combat unemployment and media interest grew. Polytechnics, providing as they do very high-level occupational education, are high status institutions in the present climate of public opinion. The media has become a kind of stakeholder in vocational education because of its influence upon public opinion.

A last group of stakeholders, those who had traditionally had great influence in general secondary education, were reluctant to embrace reform. They had high status by providing school education appropriate to 'white collar' people and they wanted to hold on to their privileged position. Inertia and comfort with the traditional would be difficult to overcome. The proposal to integrate vocational education and secondary level general education was resisted: the two were unhappy bedfellows.

## The goals of the great reform

Early in the period of the great reform, in 1974, the government set a number of important goals which parliament later, in 1978, amended into a shorter form. No analysis of the great reform would be complete without consideration of these goals.

The first goal touched upon the status of vocational education relative to general education, namely 'vocational education should be developed to provide an alternative route into higher education; one which will satisfy the changing demands of the labour market'. Despite the government's force of argument in this regard, the mind of the Finnish people would not shift. Generally, academic education is accorded a much higher status than vocational education. The committee charged with the integration of vocational and general education failed to fulfil its remit preferring instead to provide support to the separatist movement. Although it is possible to proceed to university education via the vocational education route it takes a long time and is therefore not very attractive. A fully operational polytechnic education system will make a difference by providing, as recorded above, a viable and attractive alternative to university education.

In the beginning of the 1980s the age-cohort leaving the comprehensive school was divided about 50:50 between the general education and the vocational education studies, instead of 20:80 as planned. The universities could only take less than half of the students who matriculated from the general secondary schools and as a matter of necessity therefore a system of vocational education studies based upon the general high school provision had to be introduced.

A second goal was for the development of comprehensive schooling which would enable students to pass the examination required for entry into all continuing education programmes, either academic or vocational. Progress towards achieving this goal has been more promising. Teachers (and teachers' professional organisations), perhaps partially motivated by an increase in salaries, came to terms with modifications in the curriculum. Before the reform there were two or three different levels of study available in mathematics and foreign languages which students could choose after sixth grade, but there was an inhibiting caveat. If students chose to study at the lowest levels they could not proceed to general secondary schools. After the reform there was only one level of study, but there was however more teaching support on offer to the students.

Two important outcomes stemmed from this reform. The number of student places in vocational institutions was increased so that every student who wished to could enter vocational studies either at the end of compulsory education or after completion of general secondary education. Currently there are about one-and-a-half times more places available in vocational education institutions than are taken up by those leaving comprehensive schools.

The third goal spelled out the nature of programmes to be developed for vocational education. Broad basic programmes of vocational studies which articulated with the comprehensive school provision were to be devised for all occupational sectors. Each basic programme would begin with a common foundation year but then each would have two end points: one after a further one or two years of specialised study which would culminate in a school examination, and a second after two to four years of specialised study which would culminate in a college examination.

As mentioned earlier, all vocational studies were made available to students in the secondary general schools, as well as in secondary level vocational education establishments.

Another interesting development was the integration of special education (i.e. education of people with special educational needs, the handicapped, etc.) into normal education institutions. Attainment of this goal meant that Finland now had a national system of vocational education, creditworthy and available to all. The introduction of this system also resulted in a levelling out of enrolments of boys and girls in subjects where hitherto there had been a preponderance of either sex. The percentage breakdown of students into the different areas of education provision is shown in Figure 7.5, but the proportion under polytechnics includes students enrolled in higher level courses in colleges which have still to be absorbed into the polytechnics.

## Outcomes of the great reform

For many the great reform was an exhausting process which gobbled up energy and time but which gave them a thorough understanding of the new vocational education provision as it evolved. Tired by their experience many contributors are now quite happy to see the next round of the development work passing onto younger shoulders. They are interested however in keeping alive their interests in technical and vocational education, but more from a distance than in the thick of things.

Attitudes of the media towards matters connected with vocational education have been transformed. New initiatives are more widely reported. This is also facilitated by new attitudes especially where officers of municipalities and central government are concerned. Information is now much more freely available. Taken together these changes in attitude and freely and easily accessible information have made it possible for many stakeholders to be kept aware of developments.

Looking to the future it appears most likely that the greatest influence will reside with two groups of stakeholders/process owners, those working directly in 'operations' who will want to improve the learning experiences they provide and consequently the learning outcomes, and those working in

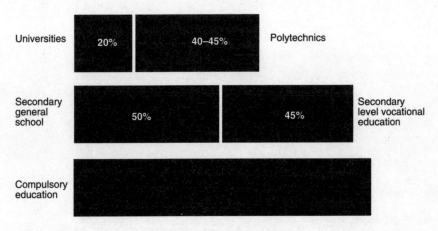

*Figure* 7.5 Division of an age group by percentage entering different education institutions

'administration' whose job it will be to see to it that the objectives for education in the various sectors are met.

The activities of these groups will be subject to tight financial controls and this will inevitably constrict involvement with stakeholders. Clear objectives will have to be set and adhered to. It will be impossible to engage in countless meetings with interested parties. Consultation will still be vitally important but it will have to be disciplined and this will necessitate changes in methods of working.

New ideas and working practices are likely to include progressing the national development programme via pilot projects. Contracts for these projects will be open to tender and progress of projects will be subject to careful monitoring. There will be open access to information about all projects. Networking and cooperation will be encouraged among everyone engaged in the delivery of vocational education or having a locus in its provision, be they national or local government officers, workforce organisations, unions and employers, social affairs bodies, municipalities and governing bodies of institutes.

Decentralisation of responsibility for the construction and implementation of curricula will necessitate the introduction of arrangements for monitoring and evaluation to operate at local level as a means of quality assurance.

In addition to the continuous monitoring mentioned above the pilot projects will be subject to evaluation both internal and external. Internal evaluations will be done by the contractors themselves and external evaluations will be supervised by those stakeholders responsible for the award of the contracts.

Above all there will be guaranteed freedom of information so that all interested parties may be kept apprised of developments.

# 8

# THE PROCESS OF CHANGE IN VOCATIONAL EDUCATION AND TRAINING IN THE UNITED STATES

*Betsy Brand*

## Introduction

Three words come to mind when discussing change in vocational technical education and training in the United States: complex, difficult, slow. I should add a fourth one, too: possible. While the United States has succeeded in making changes in the vocational education and training system, those changes have not come easily, and they are often spread out over many years and achieved only through incremental steps.

The decentralised nature of the United States' education and training system and the constitutional right of the fifty states to control education has, at times, rendered federal level leadership ineffective or counterproductive. The power of local policy boards, such as school boards or private industry councils, should not be underestimated; attempts at changes that do not cultivate local involvement will fail.

However, change can occur, and there are strategies to use to reach stakeholder groups and policy-makers at all levels of play. Building consensus happens, over time, by involving an ever-widening circle of interested parties committed to common or shared goals. As long as each stakeholder group can see the benefit of change for itself, progress can be made.

## Vocational education and training in the United States

To help provide a context for this chapter, some brief words about the vocational education and training programmes in the United States would be helpful. I hesitate to refer to vocational education and training in the United States as a 'system', meaning that federal, state and local entities, education, business and labour all work together with common goals and strategies.

Rather, we have a scattered, decentralised, unconnected amalgamation of programmes that grew up around local needs and under local control with no overarching strategy to link them together. With close to 46 million students in public schools in grades K–12 throughout the United States (projected 1996–7), the thought of organising a standardised system to reach such a large population is daunting and politically unappealing to many policy-makers. The lack of nationally accepted performance or outcome standards makes the job of creating a vocational education and training system even more difficult.

The US academic education programmes are excellent at preparing the top 25 per cent of our students who attain a baccalaureate college degree; but our high schools do very little to help the remaining 75 per cent of students who aspire to less than baccalaureate-level education. Our schools do not provide the career guidance and counselling needed by students, nor do they prepare these students for any real kind of success in the job market. In short, US students who are not headed toward a four-year post-secondary education programme are generally on their own, with no clear path to follow, and they often hold several low-wage jobs over a period of several years before they either find their niche in the economy or decide to return to school. However, this transition back to school (college) can often be difficult, as reliable and up-to-date information about programmes, the job market, and the quality of programmes is limited.

Increasingly, however, since the late 1980s, high schools and community colleges (grades 13–14) have been working to develop career education programmes to articulate grades 9–12 with years 13 and 14 at the post-secondary level, thereby encouraging more students to enter post-secondary education directly from high school, prior to moving into the labour market. These programmes, commonly called Tech Prep, are helping to lead the way in developing a more systemic approach to vocational education and training, and have prompted many communities to significantly reform their high schools.

Also, there has been increased attention focused on programmes and strategies to connect school and work and careers. These new federally funded programmes have been successful in involving more employers in programmes, and in focusing on outcome standards. However, despite national attention and federal funding for these programmes, much work remains to be done to build a true vocational education and training system in the European sense of the word.

## Who are the major stakeholders?

Identifying the major stakeholders involved with the vocational education and training programmes in the United States is a relatively easy task. Most likely, US stakeholders are very similar to stakeholders in other countries.

What is more important, however, than knowing who the stakeholders are is having a keen understanding of the role that each stakeholder group plays in the process of change, as well as the strength and power of each group in its ability to influence other stakeholders. Additionally, it is important to determine whether stakeholders are peripherally involved in the change or if they are radically or deeply affected by change. Knowing these fundamentals about stakeholder groups is key in understanding their reactions to and support of or opposition to change.

In the United States, there has been a trend not only to try to understand stakeholders better, but also to analyse a subset of stakeholders, that is customers. Since the advent of Total Quality Management and its focus on customers in the business world, the education and training system (and I use the word system, as I said before, somewhat hesitantly to describe our mass of programmes) in the United States has been trying to work out who its customers are and how to best meet their needs.

The needs and desires of customers are often very different than the needs and desires of stakeholders. For instance, let us consider the business community. Generally, the business community wants a well-trained workforce from the public education and training system, and often they see themselves as the 'buyer of the product that the public schools produce'. (This language is increasingly common among business leaders, as they purposefully try to inject business concepts of customer satisfaction into the public education system.) This 'customer' is interested in a well-trained workforce and 'products' (students/workers) with value. However, the business customer can sometimes be exempt from paying local property taxes to support the schools that produce their products because of economic development incentives. The business customer as a stakeholder is usually satisfied as long as the product is a valuable one, and may not care at all about matters of public financing of schools and the tax rates to pay for such schools.

By contrast, the general public, made up of taxpayers, a stakeholder group but not a customer, is often less concerned about the outcome from the public school system, but is more interested in the amount of taxes they pay to support local public schools. Elderly taxpayers, in particular, have frequently voted down tax increases and bond issues aimed at supporting public education, because they see no value in doing so. Elderly taxpayers are often far removed from the 'product' of the school system, and are not personally concerned about the quality of that product or using the product, but they are very concerned about the cost of supporting the schools.

Another example will point out the difference between customers and stakeholders. Many taxpayers do not want to see an education system that caters to business and prepares students just for jobs. Taxpayers in certain communities have demanded a public education system that provides a well-rounded academically-oriented education, rather than one that they perceive

139

as caving into business demands and tracking students into low-skilled and low-wage jobs.

In the United States, it is also possible to identify two major 'customers' of the public education system: the business community, which relies on schools to train their future employees; and the world of higher education, which assumes that students are interested in learning for learning's sake, rather than to gain career skills. Many hours of fruitless debate have been spent in trying to determine whether the public education system exists to prepare students for jobs or for more education, rather than the simple answer – both. But many policy-makers are only interested in listening and responding to one customer or stakeholder group, based on their prejudices and preferences, resulting in occasional bouts of schizophrenic education and training policy.

My point with these examples is to demonstrate the importance of understanding the difference between stakeholders and customers.

Effective leaders in the vocational education and training system understand that the system has multiple customers and stakeholders, with multiple views and desires. These leaders design their programmes to meet as many primary needs of their various customers and stakeholders as possible and work towards bringing these agendas together.

While the use of the word stakeholder is very common in the United States to describe individuals and groups involved in the vocational education and training programmes, some communities use the word 'partner' or 'customer' exclusively. The use of the term 'role-player' is not in current use; however, occasionally communities will use the word 'shareholder', which again evidences the influence of the business community.

In a moment, I will list the major stakeholder groups for the vocational education and training programmes in the United States. While it is fairly simple to identify the groups, each group is a complex entity, with many varied interests and subgroups. Often these smaller groups can derail majority positions or activities by their strength or through trickery. Other times, what appears to be a cohesive organisation or group can actually have so many smaller groups within that consensus is almost impossible to reach.

In managing the change process, it is critical to understand just how complex any stakeholder group is. Within groups like parents, you not only have differences based on incomes and education levels, you have cultural and racial differences, which can have an enormous influence on how parents view education and training. To assume that all parents support vocational education and training because it prepares their children for good-paying careers is a huge error, as will be discussed later. The following list is a simplification, with the understanding that each stakeholder group can be broken down into many varied subgroups.

1  *Students.* This includes students at the secondary (high school) and post-secondary levels, even though younger students are increasingly being viewed as part of the vocational education system. Students at the post-secondary level would include those involved in two- or four-year technical degree programmes, specific industry or certificate training (usually one year in length) programmes, and disadvantaged adults returning to the labour market. This last category is receiving renewed attention as the United States prepares to implement welfare reform and meet mandatory requirements to place welfare recipients in paid work positions.

2  *Parents of students.* Parents of secondary school students are an especially powerful and important group to deal with because of their attitudes (usually negative) toward vocational education and training programmes. While parents are also taxpayers, their interest is more directly focused on the success of their child.

3  *Employers.* In this category of stakeholder, I am generally referring to private employers in small, medium and large size enterprises. The public sector, which employs almost 25 per cent of American workers, should not be neglected. However, most public employers are too preoccupied with their own public policy issues as a matter of their mission to be concerned with the quality of the vocational technical education and training systems and the possible pool of employees.

4  *Taxpayers.* In the United States, most taxpayers in local communities do not have children in the public schools; and yet as much as 50 per cent of their property taxes can be used to support public education and training. Older taxpayers generally are not supportive of increases in their tax rates for education and training, while younger and middle-aged taxpayers are more likely to support increases in funding for education. Many communities have had their reform efforts put on hold because of taxpayer revolts against escalating taxes.

5  *Education and training industry.* The education and training industry includes teachers, trainers, curriculum developers, testing companies, administrators, textbook publishers and so on. Clearly each of these could be listed as an individual stakeholder, but for this chapter, I will generally refer to them as the education and training industry.

6  *Government officials and policy-makers.* This group includes elected and appointed officials at all levels of government, as well as a cadre of individuals who provide advice, guidance and ideas in policy development. The 'policy wonks' (as they are sometimes referred to in the United States) can be quite influential – holding sway over elected or appointed officials – and can be the moving force behind change.

Each of these stakeholder groups influences policy and change at the national, state and local levels, but with varying degrees of effectiveness.

Table 8.1 shows the sphere of influence of these six stakeholder groups across the national, state and local levels. From my perspective as a national policy-maker for many years, I found it helpful to map out which groups had power at which level with regard to a particular issue. By preparing a strategic map or chart, I was then able to focus my efforts more directly on the groups with which I most needed to work. (NB: this categorization is based on my fifteen years of experience in public policy, not on a research base.)

Based on my experience, I would say that in the United States, students, as stakeholders, tend to have relatively minimal influence over change in vocational education and training. Because students are generally not organised, they are unable to present unified positions to support or oppose proposals in an organised fashion. Also, many students are too young to vote and do not have any financial stake in the system, so their voice is discounted. The one arena that students have been somewhat successful in terms of 'lobbying' for change is in the area of federally financed student aid programmes. In this case, college students who receive student financial assistance have influenced Congress as to the availability of funds. However, interestingly enough, students have never organised to lobby the executive or legislative branch on issues of quality of their education!

In contrast to students, the education industry is very organised and has a very large influence on vocational education and training policy and programmes. An example of the power of the education industry controlling the system is in the selection of textbooks. Textbook selection drives curriculum and therefore has a large impact on what is taught and how it is taught. For the vocational education and training field, there are relatively few curriculum publishers that understand the need to develop high quality applied and contextual material, showing links between theory and practice. As a result, textbooks tend to be outdated and ignorant of recent technological advances, which results in outdated secondary vocational education programmes.

Textbook publishers work with teachers and administrators in several large states (Texas, New York and California) in the design of books every

*Table 8.1* Spheres of influence of stakeholder groups

| Stakeholder group | National level | State level | Local level |
|---|---|---|---|
| Students | Low | Low | Low/medium |
| Parents | Medium | Medium | High |
| Employers | High | High | High |
| Taxpayers | Low | Medium/high | High |
| Education industry | High | High | High |
| Government officials and policy-makers | High | High | High |

few years. Once these textbooks have been written to the satisfaction of the large states, they are published in quantities to meet the nationwide market. Teachers in smaller states, like Vermont or Rhode Island, effectively have no say in the design of the textbooks. Even if their state has pursued reforms independently of other states, the textbooks that are sold on the market most likely would not reflect such changes. Textbook publishers tend to design fairly bland textbooks. They do not reflect promising innovative curricula, such as applied, contextual or project-based learning or integrated teaching styles, nor do they promote change in teaching or curricula.

Another example of a powerful education industry stakeholder is the teachers' unions. The union's power to prevent change is legendary in the United States, and in many political campaigns, the teachers' unions become a symbol of all that is bad about public schools and their unwillingness to change. The education and training industry, along with teachers' unions, holds significant power at all three levels, national, state and local.

It may be of some surprise that taxpayers in the United States have little influence over the vocational education and training system at the national level. That is because the federal government provides for only about 7 per cent of the funds for education in the United States, with the states and communities providing the rest. Since the federal commitment is so small, most citizens do not focus on the national tax burden for education and training; rather they look at the tax burden closer to home, where they do exercise much greater power.

## How are stakeholders involved in the process of change?

To be somewhat glib, but also quite honest, most stakeholders are not involved in the process of changing vocational education and training programmes. Fewer and fewer Americans participate in national, state and local elections, and fewer and fewer citizens are exercising their right to vote. Also, in general, the percentage of citizens who are involved in civic, social, cultural and political organisations is declining, and there is concern that many civic and voluntary groups will dissolve through lack of support. Generally, citizens feel that their voice and vote do not count; they are cynical and tired of politics as usual.

Fundamentally, change is a complex process that takes place in a political environment. I do not mean to say that change only occurs through 'political' parties and the legislative process. Rather, I mean that to make change, one needs to understand the political environment – the perceptions, the realities, and the hopes and fears – of those around you and of the stakeholder groups that are part of the programmes or processes that are being changed. Change in a vacuum is not change, it is just talk. Change occurs when individuals and groups exhibit different behaviours, perceptions, attitudes, or desires. Getting such groups to change is a long and

143

often hard process, and takes a great deal of understanding and communication.

As many hardened politicians will say, if you can just 'push the right button' with the voters, you can get elected. But finding the right button to push, with voters or stakeholders, is a not an easy task. A whole industry, public opinion research, has grown up in the last 25–30 years in the United States to better understand voters' and consumers' preferences and willingness to change. People do not vote to change a president or buy a new kind of soap unless there is a good reason to do so. But voters and consumers often need help in understanding the reasons for changing presidents or soaps, and someone (policy-makers, community leaders, industry) must articulate those reasons simply and clearly, in a way that voters and consumers will believe and internalise.

Issues must be defined in a manner that affects stakeholders directly – at the community, family, school level, or in the wallet – in order to involve them in the process of change. A giant of American politics, former Speaker of the US House of Representatives Tip O'Neill said that all politics is local. How right he was. Most voters, consumers and stakeholders care only about what happens in their own small world, or backyard. Assuming that voters, consumers, or stakeholders have a purer, more altruistic motive for changing their behaviour usually results in a breakdown of communication and a shutdown in the process of change. (It is sad that most of us are willing to change for selfish reasons, not because it is good for the planet.) Understanding why people do or do not want to change, and being able to articulate that is one of the most important aspects of involving stakeholders in the change process. Understanding resistance to change, and working with stakeholders to overcome such resistance through persistent communication and 'checking' of the messages is also vital.

A problem faced by the vocational education and training system in the United States is apathy around these issues. Actually, most citizens would agree that schools in general need to be improved, but that their schools, their teachers, and their kids are doing all right. Many of the stakeholders of the vocational education and training programmes do not see a pressing need to change the system, so they prefer to stay with the status quo. The 'if it ain't broke, don't fix it' mentality is alive and well. Occasionally, stakeholders will see that there are significant problems to be solved, but feel unable to control the change ('I'm just one person, what can I do?') and never become engaged in the change process. This may help to explain why major school reform efforts have generally been ineffective at changing classroom and school behaviours.

While some stakeholder groups are larger and more involved than others in a change process, it is critical to check with all major stakeholder groups during a campaign of change. It also helps to build coalitions early in the process, and not create the perception that one group is 'doing' the change to another group. These points can be illustrated by some recent experiences related to proposals to consolidate, simplify and improve vocational education and training programmes in the United States.

Since 1992, efforts have been underway to reform the vocational education and training system to reduce the number of programmes, to consolidate administration of programmes at the state level, to simplify the delivery of services, to increase programme accountability through performance standards, to link school and work, to provide greater state and local control, and to create a more efficient labour market information system. To a large extent, this change was being driven by: (1) employers (the customer of the education and training system), who need better skilled workers; (2) policy-makers, who became frustrated by a confusing array of programmes that were duplicative and that lacked accountability and who needed to reduce spending; and (3) users of the vocational education and training system, who frequently got lost in the system. These groups over a period of years, came to a consensus about new programme structures, financing and accountability, contained in a legislative package called CAREERS, that as of mid-1995, was almost unanimously supported by stakeholder groups and leaders of both of our political parties.

However, as these stakeholder groups were working on the mechanics of making a better vocational education and training system, another stakeholder group – a group of conservative parents – was hearing information, much of it erroneous, about some major new programme that would change the way their children were taught in school. This parent stakeholder group came late to the discussion of reform, came with very little reliable information, but came ready to fight any changes to their children's schooling. These parents felt as though 'someone was pulling the wool over their eyes', as no one had reached out to try to educate them about the proposed changes. This stakeholder group, despite the fact that they came late to the debate and represented only a fraction of parents nationwide, succeeded in killing major reform legislation that a year earlier had been heralded as a bi-partisan reform effort with unanimous support.

What happened? What happened was that a group of conservative mums and dads heard about a big federal plan that would take their kids and push them into a vocational education programme and prepare them for a job, not for college. These parents heard that this new federal programme would be controlled by federally-determined standards, and these parents had already decided that any kind of federal standard would be a low standard with low expectations, resulting in dumbed-down curriculum and programmes. These parents heard that their kids would be tracked through high school to low-skilled jobs, and that they would be forced to learn 'vocational' skills, not academic skills. These parents heard that the programme would be controlled by Washington, D.C., and that politicians would dictate what was taught in school.

Ironically, the reform legislation sought to change all these negative stereotypes that these mums and dads believed. The reform legislation sought to turn control over to states and communities; and it sought to establish high academic and occupational learning standards. But the information that the parents received was presented in a way that fed their fears about their children's futures.

Too late did the larger group of stakeholders supporting the reform legislation realise that these parents were serious and that they were not going to go away. Efforts were made to reach out to the parent group, but by then the parents felt as though all these other groups (especially the Democratic White House, the teacher unions, and certain global businesses) had purposely kept them out of the discussions and had no real interest in working with them anyway. A level of trust, which is baseline to all communication, was severely lacking.

What could have been done differently? As a major stakeholder group, parents should have been involved early on in the discussions to change vocational education and training, but this was never done. The leaders of the change process, mostly policy-makers and government officials, should have recognised the need to reach out to all major stakeholder groups and understand what change would mean to them. In this case, it was easier for the policy-makers to work with the employer community and the education community, who were relatively willing partners in the process and easy to access.

There are a number of specific and targeted activities that can be undertaken to involve stakeholder groups in the process of change. The bottom line, however, is to communicate often and frequently, and then do it again!

Of course, to get change started, you need to identify an agent or champion of change. This champion could be an individual or a stakeholder group or a coalition of leaders from different stakeholder groups (probably the most effective model). The champions must have credibility in their own stakeholder groups, and it helps if they have credibility among many stakeholder groups (often nationally-known political leaders are able to bridge these groups).

The champions must be able to articulate a vision of what effective change would mean for the primary stakeholders, and then be able to expand that vision to other stakeholders, in order to build support. The champions do not have to be the ones to develop the platform for change; but they must be able to speak to people in a way that builds trust and credibility, and with words that hold meaning for the different stakeholder groups. The champions must also understand that success depends on the support of a broad and diverse community of stakeholders, and they must continuously reach out to involve an ever-widening circle of supporters. This means reaching out to groups that may be hostile or unknown, and therefore, champions must take certain risks as they seek to convince others to change.

Champions generally must possess a commitment to participatory management, consensus-building and democratic principles; and above all, be fair. But these individuals must also be willing to force certain actions, in violation of these principles, in order to keep the change process moving. A champion needs to know when to push matters and when to let others go, as well as have an intuitive sense of when people and groups are willing to accept change or how much change they are willing to tolerate.

Champions can appear at the national, state, or local level, or multiple champions can emerge at all or some levels from all or some of the stakeholder groups. At the local level, involvement with the change process is fairly concrete and practical. At the state and national level, interactions between stakeholder groups and their involvement in the change process becomes more diffused, less concrete, and more removed from direct service. The individuals involved in the process at the state or national level generally represent the viewpoints of a large number of individuals in their stakeholder group. The national representatives of these stakeholder groups, to effectively do their jobs, must stay in constant contact with the membership and be in touch with their current attitudes, values, beliefs and so on. At times, the national representatives of stakeholder groups are able to represent only some, not all, of their members due to conflicting positions. At other times the national representatives of stakeholder groups are completely out of touch with their members. In this case, the stakeholder group is often left out of discussions, or the national representatives do such a poor job they are replaced with someone who is in closer contact with the real feelings of the group.

At the national and state level, public hearings and meetings are frequently used as the major conduit of information-gathering, as opposed to one-on-one meetings that can occur more frequently at the local level or in smaller communities. While public hearings can be an effective manner for gathering information, the nature of the hearings does not allow for a free flow of information from the national level to the local level. This one-way flow of information often is a cause for great frustration on the part of many state and local stakeholders, and causes cynicism. And, as described above, lack of good information at the local level can result in opposition from stakeholder groups based on their ignorance of the proposed changes.

Public hearings also do not provide an opportunity for stakeholders to remain involved in the process of change. Hearings usually occur at the start of the process, and there is no effort to reconnect later on. Stakeholders should be contacted repeatedly to find out how the change is working and how it can be improved. Developing an effective feedback loop or ensuring the provision of information from the national to the state to the local level and back up again is critical in order to keep state and local stakeholders engaged and committed to change and to working in concert with national priorities.

147

Public opinion surveys are another tool used with great frequency by national policy-makers. But these surveys are impersonal and often miss the real issues of concern to stakeholders. And, stakeholders are almost never given the results of the survey they participated in, resulting, again, in a one-way flow of information and possible disaffection and cynicism.

As you move from the diffuse area of national policy-making to the state and local levels, the process of communicating with stakeholders becomes more personal, detailed and specific, and time consuming ('All politics is local'). Instead of discussing whether four or five large programmes get merged into a block grant (topics at the national level), stakeholders discuss items such as class schedules, paperwork requirements, or even sports and athletics. Often, to involve stakeholders at the local level, the discourse must be broken down into very practical issues that they deal with daily, rather than global economic and workforce policy matters.

Reaching into every community to affect vocational education and training is also difficult, but leaders of stakeholder groups can try to encourage state and local coalition-building by modelling that behaviour at the national level, and by using certain progressive or successful examples to convince others that change can be made without loss of life! As the federal government was working on the reform legislation (CAREERS), many states and communities decided to follow the federal guidelines and begin instituting their own change, ahead of schedule. Some of these progressive sites have succeeded in their efforts, and are now used as guideposts for other communities that are more timid and less certain about how to proceed.

In most of these community-led efforts to build coalitions to reform the vocational education and training system, the stakeholders decided to create a committee to study the issue and develop recommendations for change and implementation strategies. These committees usually had membership from all the stakeholder groups, and probably additional members, too. Many of the local committees were headed by a business person or someone considered to be objective, and who knows how to get things done. During the life of the committee, public hearings, town meetings, community presentations, and meetings with stakeholder groups are held. Often a public relations campaign is conducted, but the messages are more personal and reflect the concerns of the community.

Because these smaller-scale coalitions are 'close to the ground' and really just an extension of the community, they can be more effective in reaching those groups that are opposed to change or in locating any possible opponents that might not have surfaced. The champion must ensure that groups that will be most affected by change are brought into discussions as early as possible, before any decisions are made. All groups should be involved in creating options for change and enough time should be allotted for free and open discussion. While some stakeholder groups may disagree with a finding or a recommendation, if they believe they have been fairly listened to and a full partner in the process, often they will agree to a consensus position.

## What is consensus and how is it achieved?

I received the invitation to participate in the seminar about the process of change in vocational education and training just about the time the US federal government was being shut down for lack of an agreement on the 1996 budget. In this case, consensus on the budget through the political process was not achieved; however, a consensus did develop to tone down the rhetoric and re-open the government. As it turned out, consensus about the budget finally came about, only after politicians in both parties were lambasted for their juvenile behaviour and immature manner of dealing with conflict. Basically, the media embarrassed the politicians into behaving more professionally and agreeing to manage the budget process through consensus.

The United States, being a democratic society, accepts consensus, in my opinion, fairly naturally. As Americans, we accept that each individual is allowed to express his or her opinion; that each person has a vote and the responsibility to engage in the political process; and that though we may be diverse, from that diversity comes strength (*e pluribus unum* – our nation's motto). Also, Americans do not want a strong central government; they prefer decentralisation and local control over many issues, education being one of the main jurisdictions protected from federal intrusion. Because of these attitudes and values, Americans tend toward collaborative and pragmatic problem-solving, which fits well with consensus-building or management by consensus.

In the United States, the commonly understood meaning of consensus is that if everyone agrees or is willing 'to live with it', then that is consensus. If an individual or group just cannot go along with a decision, then the matter returns to a problem-solving phase. Sometimes groups will go along with a consensus decision and then object at a later time. Even in this case, most of the participants are willing to work with the group that has objections, because *e pluribus unum*: a decision that is made and supported by many people has a better chance of being widely accepted than a decision that is forced onto a group against its will. Consensus and coalition-building practices are becoming the mainstream process as more and more people work with those guidelines and understand the mutual benefits. Consensus is the 'win–win' position, and everyone walks away from the table happy.

The case for creating consensus in vocational education and training reform had been relatively successful, until, in the case of the CAREERS legislation, the conservative parent group became involved. In the United States, I think it is safe to say there is a general consensus about what changes should be made to the vocational education and training system.

The consensus is to simplify programmes, reduce bureaucracy and administrative requirements, permit greater flexibility and innovation in programmes at the state and local level, establish standards of performance for students and programmes, use more applied and contextual teaching and learning, build more effective linkages between schools and businesses that permit more work-based learning opportunities, develop greater career awareness and guidance, and connect programmes into a seamless system.

Achieving this consensus did take years, and there are still major stakeholders (conservative parents and the university system, for example) that do not completely buy into the changes. (More work to keep us all busy.) The impetus to develop this consensus agenda came primarily from the business community with a plea for more highly skilled workers. Teachers also joined in as they saw from firsthand experience that students were bored and dropping out of school because classes were irrelevant and school was leading nowhere.

Fortuitously, the visions for change and reform at the national, state and local levels were similar enough that they supported and amplified each other. The reasons that stakeholder groups at these three levels got involved in reform efforts differed to some extent, but the goals they were after were quite similar. The fact that the federal, state and local level concerns aligned so closely helped in the development of a consensus position.

An example of this alignment relating to the consolidation/simplification proposals follows. There was a general consensus that the number of vocational education and training programmes should be reduced or consolidated. At the local level, this consensus developed because consumers and clients became increasingly frustrated in trying to sort out the myriad of federal, state, and local programmes, and in determining eligibility, services, and so on. At the state level, governors and state officials were frustrated by the complex administrative requirements of multiple programmes. Several very similar programmes would often use slightly different terminology, creating the need for multiple tracking and accounting systems, rather than a single, comprehensive system. This was documented in various research papers written by the National Governors' Association.

At the national level, policy-makers were faced with decreasing budget resources, that argued for programme consolidation or downsizing. The Congress also began to see the overlap between agencies and programmes that occurred as they continued to expand programmes indiscriminately over the years without a strategic plan or vision. Lastly, a major report by the US General Accounting Office tallied over 154 vocational education and training programmes, valued at $25 billion, at fourteen agencies, thus providing weighty facts and figures to validate the need for consolidation. All of these reasons fed into the development of a consensus position that vocational education and training programmes should be consolidated with funding going to states and localities in a more flexible manner.

As national, state and local stakeholders began to talk to each other about their concerns, it became clear that all were headed in the same direction, for slightly different reasons. The convergence of opinion about the need to simplify and consolidate programmes was overwhelming. Even members of the education industry, which would normally fight reductions in programmes and dollars, felt pressure from its constituency to make life simpler and improve services.

Consensus can be achieved most rapidly if there is some alignment in stakeholder views at the national, state and local levels. In the example above, there was alignment of opinion, albeit stemming from different symptoms, that led to an agreement to consolidate and simplify programmes. Sometimes this alignment of opinions occurs at roughly the same time, as it did in the example above, in which case change can happen more quickly. However, if one level of stakeholders has to convince stakeholders at other levels, change obviously will take longer and be more difficult.

Finding champions in each stakeholder group – or in the groups with the most influence at each level – is critical. Table 8.1 (see p. 142) would point to the importance of involving employers, the educational industry and government officials at all levels; taxpayers and parents at the state and local level; and students (including adult students) at the local level. Identifying strong champions with similar goals in each of these spheres will speed consensus.

There also often exists an informal network of opinion-makers and stakeholders who know each other and talk together about what changes should be made and how to make them. These informal groups, usually based on friendship or other alliances (clubs, college alumni, and so on), exist at the national, state and local levels. Influencing and using these informal networks can be a very effective means of promoting change and reducing the amount of time required for stakeholder groups to support change.

Champions can also be associated with unique, innovative programmes that test some new theory or practice. The individuals associated with the innovative programmes can share their experiences, outcomes and findings with other stakeholders as they make a case for change. Innovative programmes that are then substantiated through research can be used as real-life examples of how people have gone through a successful change. This 'storytelling' by using personal examples is a very effective way to help stakeholders grasp the notion of change, understand where they fit in, and what it means for them.

An example of this is the 'Tech Prep' programme, a reform programme that links high school with community college and prepares students for careers in the fields of technology, engineering, science, business and health. Several communities started Tech Prep programmes to reform their vocational education and training programmes, and served as the 'guinea pigs'

151

for others to watch. The early communities knew that they were being watched and often made extra efforts to involve the right people and find ways of succeeding. Once several communities were able to describe their experience and success with Tech Prep, and validated through respected research, other stakeholders were more willing to throw their support behind similar reform efforts. Following several years of experimentation at the community level, enough support had developed for this reform effort that it was included in the Carl D. Perkins Vocational and Applied Technology Education Act as a separately funded programme in 1990.

Consensus takes time to develop. Perhaps one of the reasons for the breadth of consensus in the United States with regard to reforming vocational education and training is that these changes have now been discussed for enough years that people feel comfortable with them. When new ideas are presented to any group or individual, most will react with wariness, disinterest, fear, or even hostility. It really is quite rare to find individuals or groups that just can't wait for change. Over time, however, after having an opportunity to think about the ramifications of a certain change, the groups may come to see that the changes are not all bad, and may even be good.

Lastly, consensus is achieved through creating trust and effective and consistent communication between the champions or agents of change and with the field of stakeholders. While different messages can be given to different stakeholder groups about why a change is good, the underlying values, principles and goals espoused by the change agents and champions must be consistent. For instance, on the issue of standards-based vocational education and training, it is all right to tell employers that standards will result in better employees, hence greater productivity; and it is all right to tell taxpayers that standards will lead to greater accountability and quality within the system, hence better use of public tax dollars. The message is tailored to each group's interest and concerns, but they are true and consistent attributes of a standards-based education system.

Any effort to resort to trickery or misrepresentation will almost always be found out, and will usually have the impact of destroying any trust that existed between individuals or groups. Once trust is destroyed, it is hard to win back and often the group or individuals who lie will never be accepted by their peers and colleagues again.

The media has a major role to play in the development of consensus, whether or not it is even aware of it. Using the public media to carry your story to the general public or a particular segment can help you to build consensus by reaching people that you cannot personally reach and talk to. The media often has to be the messenger in the United States, for there often is no other way to communicate with so many millions of Americans. Of course, it is important to ensure that the media carry the right message, or public opinion can quickly be turned against change.

Using mass media to develop a consensus across a wide spectrum of people or groups can be problematic. As discussed earlier, it is important to tailor messages to groups so that they get meaning from the message. Trying to create a message that can 'speak' to millions of Americans on a subject as complex as education, training, economic development, and teaching and curriculum can be very taxing, and may result in a message that is so watered down to meet the common denominator, that it is useless.

Using trade press and media and tailoring messages (through direct mail, for example), can be more effective in attempts to describe complicated change agendas. Usually professionals who read the trade press have some degree of respect for those publications and are willing to accept the information as non-biased or non-political. For these reasons, using focused and targeted media is usually effective in reaching specific stakeholder groups. Placing editorials or opinion pieces by well-respected leaders of stakeholder groups can help sway other stakeholders. Similarly, positive articles about communities or groups that have attempted some type of reform is helpful for others to learn how to get started.

## Epilogue

Legislation to consolidate and simplify vocational education and training programmes is still pending in the US Congress. After the CAREERS bill died at the end of 1996, congressional elections were held and plans were made by some to introduce a different legislative proposal that was more sensitive to the conservative parents' concerns. In the House of Representatives, two bills were introduced: one bill to update and improve the Carl D. Perkins Vocational and Applied Technology Education Act, and another bill to consolidate the adult job training programmes. By separating out the two bills, the connection between education and training had been broken, and the parent groups seemed placated that the vocational education programmes will not be driven by labour market demands, but rather by academic learning.

However, the US Senate decided to introduce reform legislation that keeps the Perkins Act (vocational education) attached to the adult job training programmes, which causes the parent groups great consternation. At this point, it is unclear when the legislation will be approved.

Despite the legislative logjam, the consensus that I described around reform in vocational education and training continues to grow. Governors and state and local officials are taking the lead in changing their programmes and simplifying, consolidating and improving them. Also, while national legislation has not yet been approved, the Congress did approve a smaller measure permitting states and communities to apply for waivers from various federal laws to permit consolidation, and reduce duplication and paperwork to better serve clients. These waivers have effectively bypassed the need for federal legislation in some states and communities, and are proving to be very popular and effective. Because they are locally driven, rather than coming down from the federal government, community groups have been more willing to accept the change they have brought. Waiver authority in these and additional programmes will continue to grow and flourish – perhaps negating the need for a national overhaul of vocational education and job training programmes.

## Consensus in the United States and other countries

Following the discussion at the seminar on the change process in vocational education and training, it was clear that most of the participants did indeed have a concept of consensus that was similar and that seemed to fit the 'I can live with it' standard. And most participants discussed similar outreach and information-sharing activities that must occur in order to get stakeholder buy-in.

Perhaps the greatest difference that struck me during the discussion was the amount of control that centralised governmental bodies in certain countries were able to exert over the change process. Because the United States has less of a centralised and powerful government than many other nations, it was fascinating to hear how the governmental structure controlled each step of the process. Most striking of all was the case of Singapore, whose government basically told people to change or else! In Singapore, consensus did not seem to really exist as from free will, but as in reaction to government control. (Of course, the 'I can live with it' standard works if you are being threatened and you have no other choice.)

It was also interesting to note the amount of time that several centralised governments spent in planning for change, which is usually not the way it happens in the United States. Several countries, notably Finland, spent years planning out reform strategies for their vocational education and training system, before implementing the reforms. While Americans could never bear to spend so much time planning (we want to 'do'), the planning did serve the purpose of informing the Finnish citizens as to the proposed changes and succeeded in gaining their support. So while a planning process may seem too lengthy to Americans, it could actually result in greater buy-in from diverse groups, which would be a great benefit.

Most nations do not have such a diverse population as the United States does, and so the values of the stakeholder groups were more homogenous than is often the case in America. As other countries are becoming more diversified, there will be an increased focus on developing consensus between groups that have diametrically opposed belief and value systems, making the change process much more difficult. The experiences of the United States in this area may be of help to other nations.

Finally, all participants agreed that the process of change is a complex human activity, that it is itself constantly changing and evolving. To reform a major system like vocational education and training involves multiple players and partners throughout society and the economy, all with different needs and desires. Adding to the complexity is the fact that when change occurs, it carries with it very great emotions. We are not just dealing with laws and regulations, but with how people relate to each other, and what are their values and beliefs. Any political or government official who thinks change can occur by just rearranging words on paper will not be in that position for long; nor will any real change occur. Change is about capturing the hearts and minds of the people you are working with and helping them to find a better path to the future.

Creating meaningful and lasting change is not a science, but an art. That is clear in any country.

# References

## Reports

Commission on the Skills of the American Workforce (1990) *America's Choice: High Skills or Low Wages!* Rochester, NY: National Center on Education and the Economy

National Governor's Association (1997) *Restructuring and Reinventing*, Washington, D.C.: State Workforce Development Systems

US Department of Education (1996) *Condition of Education*, Washington, D.C.: US Government Printing Office

US General Accounting Office (1993) *Multiple Employment Programs: National Employment Training Strategy Needed*, Washington, D.C.

—— (1994a) *Multiple Employment Training Programs: Overlapping Programs Can Add Unnecessary Administrative Costs*, Washington, D.C.

—— (1994b) *Multiple Employment Training Programs: Conflicting Requirements Hamper Delivery of Services*, Washington, D.C.

## Federal legislation – existing

Carl D. Perkins Vocational and Applied Technology Education Act
Job Training Partnership Act

## Federal legislation – proposed

S. 1186, Workforce Investment Partnership Act (1997)
H.R. 1853, Carl D. Perkins Vocational-Technical Education Act Amendments of 1997
H.R. 1617, S. 143 Workforce and Career Development Act of 1996 (CAREERS)

# 9

# THE PROCESS OF CHANGE IN VOCATIONAL EDUCATION AND TRAINING

## The South African experience

### *Ian Bellis*

### The earlier context

In South Africa, the process of change, in what in the title of this book is referred to as 'vocational education and training', is rooted in the processes of our dramatic, profound and wide-ranging political, social and economic reconstruction. These changes, however, are taking place at an uneven pace. Very intensive processes, leading to policy and legislation, followed by struggles to effect the changes, in terrain that is permeated with deep and passionate feeling and enormous structural and administrative complexities. These realities are part of the legacy of our political, and therefore educational, history.

The origins of what needed to change lie in our past. The nature of the processes and the shape of current change are a reflection of a society struggling to achieve a democracy which not only reshapes structures, but attempts to redress injustices and imbalances and underdevelopment. A more settled and detailed shape, in terms of the new vision for education and training, lies in the future.

In the context of South African political and social history, one has to realise how thoroughly our education and training structures were the expression of an overwhelmingly dominant political ideology. This ideology was itself grounded in the particular cultural and politico-religious philosophy of the party that governed from 1948 to 1994. That this was so, is not mere observation of fact. It also reflects the painful and demoralising realities and experiences of the black majority of the population. Education and training reflected all the inequities, all the imbalances, all the injustices and (specifically to the issue of this discussion) all the 'separatenesses' of the governing ideology.

In our educational past, that separateness was represented in a plethora of education departments reflecting divisions that were political, geographical and racial. It was also represented in traditional patterns and in legislation that limited the vocational education component to providing ready access to the white community and virtually no access to the black community. This applied equally to craft, trade and technical qualifications, apprentice-ships and careers. Some degree of change in this area took place over several years prior to the General Election of 1994. Significant as those changes were in terms of assumptions and value systems, they represented an extremely small shift numerically. It was also of significance that over a period of at least twenty years the business community, especially the organ-isations requiring trade and technical skills, had been pressing for changes in legislation around jobs and, therefore, around training and the educational foundations of their employees.

Throughout this century there has been a marked divide within the polit-ically and economically dominant white group in which so-called 'academic' schooling has been seen as that to which all young people aspire (or ought to aspire). Vocational education therefore, with naturally a few notable excep-tions, has been seen as the field of those who have 'failed' academically. This opprobrium did not apply to those who, having been highly successful at school, proceeded to university to study in technical and scientific fields. The same applies, albeit to a lesser extent, for those who were not quite so successful at school and who studied in these same scientific and technical directions at Technikons. The technical college sector, which catered for those who had completed nine years of schooling, provided the vocational education home for the next three years' schooling in technical, craft and trade fields, and, increasingly, in commercial fields for those viewed within the education system and in the public mind as less capable.

This hierarchical structure (and its related snobberies), plus the domina-tion of 'white' education by those associated culturally and/or politically with the National Party government, and compounded by the exclusion of black students (until 'black' technical colleges and Technikons were created), had a number of highly significant consequences:

1   The attitude of whites towards vocational or technical education was readily adopted by the rapidly growing urban black population. Aspirations (even within the structures of apartheid) were geared towards 'white-collar' jobs.
2   A lack of teachers in fundamental subjects, such as mathematics and science, resulted in the vast majority of black secondary school pupils taking subjects that prepared them for neither tertiary academic nor tertiary vocational education and training. While the large informal sector of the economy gives striking evidence of technical skills and innovativeness, little of this is captured in either the education

structures or the work undertaken at community level by NGOs, voluntary bodies and church/welfare organisations (again with some notable exceptions).

3   Both the perceived status hierarchy of 'academic', 'technical' and 'vocational' educational institutions, and the fact that (in terms of usual requirements) there were lower qualification levels for staff, meant that, on the whole, the vocational sector was staffed by very conservative, traditionalist and often less capable personnel. This could be seen both as cause and effect of much in the system.

4   A consequence of these realities and perceptions has been that, in general, both the academic and business communities have held a very low opinion of many institutions in the vocational field such as the technical college sector and some Technikons. So low an opinion that many would wish to see technical colleges abolished, either because they have failed or because this sector reflects some of the most damaging and unappealing aspects of the apartheid regime. Once again there are several outstanding exceptions to this general observation. The fact that there are presently 136 technical colleges and 15 regional training centres (basic trade/vocational/craft) is held by some to represent a physical resource and, potentially, rich sites for vocational education.

5   A good deal of industry-based training has been undertaken over many decades, but the range of quality in this training has been from extremely good to perfunctory and ineffective. Some of this industry training has been integrated into formal vocational education and trade qualifications, while other training has been company-bound, frequently restricting the mobility of the employee. A limitation of this type of training has been the fact that many employees have not achieved a level of general education and/or capability in English or Afrikaans (the major languages in the conduct of business in terms of documentation) that enables them to take part in the more formal developmental programmes typically offered by those organisations. Thus the language issue (or more broadly 'literacy' regarding language, numbers, technology) has become a major part of addressing the whole area of vocational education.

The situation regarding vocational education and training then was one demanding radical reconstruction. Our educational history was discriminatory and unequal. The philosophy of Christian National Education propagated by the National Party government, and frequently described as 'not Christian, not national and not education', had created enormous problems and much tragedy. The confusion of qualifications – variously accredited, of uneven standard, of unclear designations, without sensible articulation – demanded attention.

With these issues in mind the NTB's Committee 2 saw the need to address, *inter alia*, the following needs:

- To simplify the structure of qualifications
- To develop relevant and responsive learning
- To introduce a fair assessment system
- To establish a system that is dynamic and flexible
- To promote access to learning
- To provide a wide variety of routes to qualification
- To encourage more people to participate in further education and training

## Some developments relating to VET since 1990

In this section of the paper I will set out, briefly, the issues surrounding a number of initiatives that have led to the reconstruction of education and training in a new set of legislation. The structures to put this legislation into effect are currently being developed.

In the crises in the country during the late 1980s and the early 1990s, a forum was formed to discuss and seek ways out of the chaos in education and specifically in 'black' education. This body, the National Education Forum (NEF) was brought into being as a result of great pressure by the business community to bring the National Party government and the 'education community' (both that which represented the governing powers and that which represented the 'democratic opposition') to the table. This forum had been given the assurance by the president, Mr F.W. de Klerk, that no major moves in the education field would be made without consultation. Within weeks, and without consultation with all the relevant stakeholders, the then Minister of Education announced the restructuring of education in an *Educational Renewal Strategy* (ERS; 1992). This had much to do with administrative structure and nothing to do with the fundamental problems in the broad system of education and training. The strong reaction this move provoked, fuelled the fires of determination to bring about change.

This type of approach, of producing policy or strategy documents directly from the bureaucratic structures of the day, was typical of government style. It was similar to a *National Training Strategy* that was developed in the late 1980s and early 1990s by a government-appointed commission with very limited credibility and consisting of largely like-minded people. This document was never seriously debated, and in particular, entirely excluded powerful and important sections of the trade union movement. The Congress of South African Trade Unions (COSATU), in very clear terms, refused even to comment on the distributed document as it had never been party to the discussion, let alone the decisions and recommendations. This rejection marked, in my view, a turning point in perceiving that the way of bringing about change in education as in politics would have to become inclusive and participative.

In the same year as the ERS, namely 1992, a research project, broadly under an ANC (African National Congress) umbrella but involving a wide range of knowledgeable and active people resulted in a series of publications which became known as the NEPI study – *National Education Policy Investigation*. This work proved seminal in many respects and covered the entire spectrum of education and training.

The ANC published, via their Education Department, *A Policy Framework of Education and Training* in January 1994. In this document a National Qualification Framework (NQF) was proposed.

As a contribution to the discussion and debate, and an important one, COSATU brought the results of their own Participative Research Project on Human Resource Development. This project had run prior to and concurrently with the early work of the National Training Board (NTB).

An investigation had been started in 1993 by what became known as the NICE Trust (National Investigation into Community Education). A first draft of their proposals was published in January 1994 and a final document, the NICE Report, in August 1995, titled *A Framework for the Provision of Adult Basic and Further Education and Training*. This group has become known as the College Sector Coalition and is a major stakeholder and influence in, particularly, the further education sector.

Yet another document, produced by the South African Institute of Distance Education (SAIDE) proposed an open learning model. This approach was consistent with that of the ANC, which proposed a structure to be known as the National Open Learning Academy (NOLA) which supports the notion of lifelong learning – an important item in the thinking of all who support the new approach. Distance learning is destined to become an increasingly important and very large component of the learning system.

Initiated in 1992, with work more effectively begun in 1993, a major project was in progress under the auspices of the then Minister of Manpower and the NTB. This consisted of a Task Team, to whom reported eight committees, each responsible for researching an aspect of education and training. Committee 2 of this project had proposed and developed the notion of an integrated NQF in its Committee Report of November 1993. The final edited document of the Task Team, *Discussion Document on a National Training Strategy*, was published in April 1994.

It can be deduced from the above that there was a considerable amount of investigation and a large number of contributions to the re-thinking of education and training in South Africa. The result of this effort has been White Papers in education and training, a number of draft bills, and finally legislation regarding education, a South African Qualifications Authority (SAQA) and a National Qualification Framework (NQF).

## The nature and shape of vocational education and training

It is of the greatest significance to note that the National Training Board's initial brief was to research and make proposals regarding a National Training Strategy – as the title of its discussion document confirms. However, the research (which was a participative process) soon moved from a consideration of *training* to a consideration of *vocational education and training* and finally to the entire spectrum of *education and training*. Hence the nature of the proposals regarding a National Qualification Framework and the subsequent related legislation.

So marked was the shift and so inclusive the process and so strong the movement towards (in the view of most) an *integrated approach* and (in the view of others) towards an *integrated system*, or even towards both *approach and system* (among whom I count myself) that any notion of a separate vocational education and training domain almost disappeared while the discussions were in progress. This integrated approach has been reflected in the fact that much of the senior level decision-making and formulation has been taking place through the Inter-Ministerial Working Group – a group representing the structures and concerns of both the Departments of Education and of Labour. Traditionally the domain of education of all types and at all levels was the province of the Departments of Education while training was the province of the Department of Labour (previously Manpower). This is still the case.

Personally, I have some concern at retaining a clearly demarcated vocational education and training (VET) sector for a number of reasons. These are reasons regarding the nature of learning as well as traditional practices, all of which – in the South African context – tend to reduce the quality of learning, and the richness of development. This sharp demarcation has also tended to increase mechanistic approaches and widen the gulf between so-called 'academic' learning and qualifications, on the one hand, and 'vocational' learning and qualifications on the other. I am aware that it is not the purpose of this paper to explore this particular issue. I am also aware of the impact that the German 'dual system' has had on some pockets of practice and of vocational education and training. With this emphasis, the term *vocational* has a very specific connotation.

The central importance of the relationship between work and learning for the adult learner is, in my view, one of the major driving forces in the developments referred to thus far. I am, nevertheless, strongly of the opinion that the lack of clarity about concepts and terms such as 'academic', 'vocational', 'technical' and 'general' attached to education and training leads to muddled and less effective structures, processes and curricula.

The fact that reference to a vocational education sector appears to have been lost is confirmed in the NQF structure as formulated at present. This shows some vocational training in the adult learning component at the same NQF levels as the first nine years of schooling; shows pre-tertiary vocational education and vocational training as at the same levels as secondary schooling in the further education component; and shows tertiary vocational education in the same component as *academic* tertiary studies. The College Sector Coalition would also view vocational education and training as being widely distributed in all three components and across many sources of provision as is stated above. Despite this, there remains a marked distinction regarding those institutions that provide vocational education.

## Change processes – policy processes

I make no apology for devoting a substantial section of this paper to the contextual issues dealt with thus far. The processes towards achieving consensus regarding change in vocational education and training in South Africa cannot be understood in either their origins or subsequent development without a consideration of those occurrences and those issues.

While the contributions (reports, proposals, discussion documents *et al.*) followed their own processes, there do seem to be several elements in common. These common elements relate not only to the actual processes (which will be described later) but specifically as to how these processes affect the dynamics of change, and of policy-making as an instrument of change.

One of the widely used diagrammatic representations of effective change sets out the change components as:

|          | pressure for change |
|----------|---------------------|
| *plus*   | clear, shared vision |
| *plus*   | the capacity for change |
| *plus*   | articulated, planned action |

will result in successful change

It is argued that the absence of any one of these will militate against effective change being achieved. A lack of strong pressure for change (which would include political will) will result in the change issue becoming a less urgent priority. A lack of a clear shared vision will result in a series of general initiatives in the direction of change but, through lack of direction, will not produce continued effort. A lack of capacity for change will mean much planned activity followed by little progress and no ultimate success. A lack of planned action will result in haphazard, unintegrated effort and no sustained progress. There has been evidence of deficiency in each of these areas in the South African process.

The literature in the area of policy-making in general, and policy-making for education and training in particular, has demonstrated, in the opinion of this writer, that change is more complex in its achievement than either the policy theorists or the change protagonists would lead us to believe. There is also good evidence that policy-making in Africa – as in other 'Third World' or developing countries – has a different character from policy-making processes in the more mature democracies.

Models for structural change through policy change vary and it may be constructive to set some of these alongside each other in conjunction with the change pattern just mentioned. This is tabulated on p. 166. The literature and experience, and here I refer to the South African experience, seems to indicate that such patterns of structural change via policy change may follow exactly or approximately one or other of these approaches either consciously or simply by selection of a *modus operandi* for change without formally determining a model to be used. In this latter case one would be interpreting the events and processes in hindsight, which is very much the nature of this short paper!

In this regard Porter, with reference to Kingdon, comments as follows:

> The separate streams of problems, policies, and politics each have lives of their own –
>
> - Problems are recognised and defined according to processes that are different from the ways in which policies are formulated and political events unfold.
> - Policy alternatives are developed according to their own criteria of selection, whether or not they are solutions to recognised problems or sensitive to political considerations.
> - Political events flow along their own often unpredictable schedule, whether or not they are related to problems or policy proposals.
>   There come times, however, when these three streams are joined. An event in the political stream, such as a change in Administration, calls for different policy directions. At that point, proposals that fit the political event come to the fore and are coupled to the prevailing climate. Or a pressing problem demands attention and a policy proposal is coupled to that problem as its solution.
>
> (Porter 1995: 23–4)

It would seem arguable that the stage and classical models and the change process pattern are linear both in conception and execution, whereas the multiple streams model contains the possibility of an iterative and, in my view, richer process. This multiple streams approach could well be used to inform, and thereby modify, the more linear approaches. This, in my view is what we are experiencing now in South Africa – by default if not by design.

# The bases of the change processes

*Pressures – political will – processes*

It was evident from the time of the release of Nelson Mandela that (then) President de Klerk was preparing the country for the certainty of major political change. The result of that announcement on 6 February 1990 and the subsequent unbanning of the ANC and other political groups was that processes that had begun among groups in opposition now had a different standing. They were widely perceived to be no longer opposition views but the probable view of an incoming ANC-dominated government of national unity.

The first basis for substantive change then was the fact that there would be not just what Porter and Kingdon refer to as a 'change of administration' (even in the American sense of 'administration') but a radical reconstruction of all major political, economic, social and educational systems and structures, institutions and processes. This shift in political reality had enormous impact on the way interest groups formed and re-formed around the processes of change in education and training. Almost overnight it was realised by many (but by no means all) that that which had been perceived by the majority of whites as the more radical views, were the views of those likely to become the political leaders, the managers and the administrators in a new dispensation.

In the emerging groupings then were the ANC; its political allies among the trade unions – notably COSATU; NGOs, who in the main were working with and for groups who were disadvantaged and discriminated against; educationalists within the 'democratic opposition'. In terms of capacity this group was considerably enhanced by the number of returning exiles who had, in many cases, gained considerable exposure to international debate and experience, and had acquired advanced academic qualifications.

As part of an already established grouping one would have anticipated the providers such as the Technikons and technical colleges to have a clear standpoint. It would seem however that their response was ambivalent: first, because of their history; second, because they wished to play a role in the new dispensation; but, third, because they appeared uncertain both of the nature of that future and the role they would play in the processes.

Another established group was that of the educational authorities of the old dispensation. In the processes that took place under the aegis of the NTB, their role appeared cautious, defensive, suspicious of their territory being invaded and taken over by those who, in their perception, may have known a great deal about 'training' but little about 'education'. This concern expressed much of the polarisation of the processes, the approaches and the personnel of what, until now, had been perceived as two worlds. The members representing this group did, however, go along with what was emerging, even if somewhat reluctantly.

The National Training Board (NTB) could also be viewed as an established grouping. While it was in fact part of the earlier regime, it had recently had new leadership appointed who adopted inclusive processes, and it became one of the leaders of change, and its document one of the major catalysts for new policy.

A grouping, though loose and informal, which exerted powerful pressure was that representing the business community. This grouping had been instrumental in the creation and functioning of the NEF (National Education Forum) and the NETF (National Education and Training Forum) which grew out of the NEF. With the access business had to international developments, processes and people in the entire labour, education and training field, it became a powerful influence.

Thus the various constituencies emerged and they became stakeholders both as the grouping they represented and through committed and effective individuals. It is evident that they represented a wide spectrum of differing ideologies, points of departure, perception and agendas. It was also evident that earlier assumptions and perceptions of each other, distrust and suspicion, enthusiasm and reserve, excitement at impending change and anxiety over the nature of that change, contributed to relationships between the various groupings. These relationships and attitudes ranged from collaborative and supportive to adversarial and defensive.

Some of these stakeholders 'emerged', others were consciously identified and formally brought into the process. Most of them functioned in the way they typically would as part of their own usual activities. This fact had a marked effect on processes towards achieving consensus throughout all stages of analysis to the later analysis of exploration, formulation and recommendation. (This will be discussed more fully shortly.)

The fact that there was this marked diversity meant that the first stage of the process – variously identified earlier as the 'pressure for change', 'problem analysis' or 'agenda setting' of the change/policy process (see Table 9.1) – was considerably enriched. In retrospect, it is also clear that the nature and quality of the outcomes of these early phases is a direct function of both the way in which the process is facilitated and how accurately and inclusively all relevant stakeholders have been identified and involved.

A most important basis of the change processes was one that emerged in the early stage of most of the independent projects but was, quite deliberately, made to be the focus of the NTB process. Here I, as observer and participant, wish to introduce a more personal note. My own involvement began with an invitation to facilitate the work of Committee 2. This committee was charged with proposing a national strategy for, initially, vocational education and training and, subsequently, as the process progressed, for education and training as a whole. The committee had, at that stage, begun its discussions and believed it was ready to start considering possible frameworks that would be central to the strategy. There was,

*Table 9.1* Descriptions of the change/policy process

| Change process | Stage model | Classical model | Multiple streams model |
| --- | --- | --- | --- |
| Pressure for change | Identification of policy problems | Problem analysis | Recognise problems |
| | Agenda setting | Policy option formulation | |
| Clear shared vision | Policy proposals | | |
| Capacity for change | Adoption and legitimisation through political action of the government | Policy option advocacy and option evaluation | Generate proposals for policy change |
| Actionable steps | | Planning | Engage in political activities |
| | Implementation | Implementation | |
| | Evaluation of programmatic implementation and impact | Evaluation | |

in addition, a markedly confrontational climate with widely differing standpoints, as referred to earlier, being dogmatically and (at times) vehemently expressed. Movement towards consensus seemed unlikely as the clearly evident ideological standpoints appeared irreconcilable. It became imperative that we step back from structure and explore and establish principle. It is characteristic of much in our political, business and sporting history that we move from one failed or ineffective structure to another structure that is perceived to be 'better'. It was necessary to interpose between the existing, failed structures and future structures a phase of rigorous conceptual thinking before identifying and examining options.

It is interesting that the principles identified, explored, clarified, defined, refined and finally unanimously agreed upon, became not only the basis for the NQF as eventually formulated and proposed, but also became the very principles that guided the process of policy analysis, formulation and so on. They came to be seen as valid also for guiding the planning and implementation of the legislation, the structures, the programmes that will follow. They are part of what is now assumed to be the basis for this kind of activity and for such diverse processes as management (in business and in education and training), curriculum development and employer–employee relations.

The principles enunciated are set out in Figure 9.1 (read from bottom to top). The relationships between the principles and processes are of great importance, as is the sequence implied, for both development activities and implementation activities.

These principles were worked on by the committee very intensely and intensively using draft documents and definitions that had been drawn up

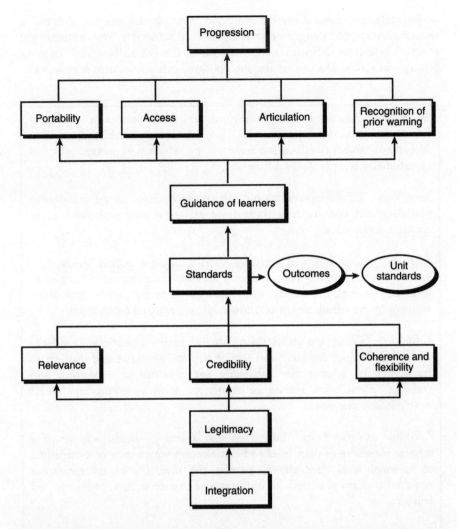

*Figure 9.1* Principles for the integration of education and training – the NQF

on the basis of work done in South Africa, Australia and New Zealand and my own work in areas related to the notion of 'competence' in education and training. The summarised statement of these principles is set out on p. 168. The processes towards consensus were, and are, based on the fact that unless they are integrated and reflect *integration*, include fully representative *participation* (legitimacy), and clearly are *relevant* to all stakeholder concerns, they do not achieve *credibility*. All processes are aimed at proposals, policy notions, structures that reflect *coherence and flexibility*. (These two were deliberately construed as constituting one principle and not two because of the unquestionable danger of striving for, or achieving, one without the other.) These brief definitions were set out in the NTB's National Training Strategy Initiative Document and incorporated into subsequent legislation.

*Integration*   Education and training should form part of a system of human resources development which provides for the establishment of an *integrated approach* to education and training which is expressed in terms of nationally acceptable qualifications.

*Legitimacy*   Education and training should provide for the *participation* in planning and coordination thereof for all significant stakeholders, to ensure transparency.

*Relevance*   Education and training should be and remain *relevant* to national development needs; industry and service sector needs; regional, local and community needs; individual development needs; and needs relating to the advancement of knowledge, science and technology.

*Credibility*   Education and training should have international *credibility* and credibility for industry and service sectors, providers and learners in its ability to achieve the nationally agreed aims for education and training. These aims should be consistent with economic and social development priorities.

*Coherence and flexibility*   Education and training should adhere to a *coherent framework* of principles and certification which may be established at national level, but should permit the *flexibility* of interpretation required to meet the needs of industry and service sectors, providers and learners.

*Standards*   Standards of education and training should be expressed in terms of a *nationally agreed framework* and nationally and internationally accepted *outcomes*.

*Guidance of learners*   Education and training should provide for the guidance of learners by persons who meet *nationally recognised standards for educators and trainers*.

*Recognition of prior learning*   Education and training should through assessment give *credit to prior learning* obtained through formal, non-formal and informal learning and/or experience.

*Access*   *Access* to appropriate levels of education and training should be provided for all prospective learners in a manner which facilitates progression.

*Portability*   Education and training should provide for learners to *transfer* their credits or qualifications from one learning institution and/or employer to another.

*Articulation*   Education and training should provide for learners, on successful completion of *accredited prerequisites*, to move between components of the delivery system.

*Progression*   Education and training should ensure that the framework of qualifications permits individuals to *progress* through the levels of national qualifications via different appropriate combinations of the components of the delivery system.

These principles and processes were given expression in terms of a vision statement which looked towards 'a human resources development system in which there is an integrated approach to education and training and which meets the economic and social needs of the country and the development needs of the individual' (National Training Strategy Initiative 1994: 6).

This vision (as the second component of the change process) was described in terms of an overall strategy, namely: 'Education and training must empower the individual, improve quality of life and contribute towards development targets in the national economic plan through a National Qualification Framework.'

The structure of the proposed NQF is reproduced as Figure 9.2.

## Consensus then – consensus now!

It has been noted earlier that consensus became easier to achieve once a basis of common principles had been agreed upon. This was particularly true of the groups that had widely diverse membership. It is probably true that other (earlier) consensus processes came about on the basis of common sets of assumptions (as with the ANC or the COSATU component of the trade union movement) and on an established *modus operandi* in dealing with, communicating with, and consulting with their own constituencies.

No formal definition of consensus was determined but in several of the working committees it was decided that consensus would have been achieved when all confirmed their agreement, not merely when there was broad general agreement.

This aspect of a grouping's usual or traditional *modus operandi* affected a

169

| NQF level | Band | Types of qualifications and certificates | |
|---|---|---|---|
| 8 | Higher education and training band | Doctorates<br>Further research | |
| 7 | | Higher degrees<br>Professional qualifications | |
| 6 | | First degrees<br>Higher diplomas | |
| 5 | | Diplomas<br>Occupational certificates | |
| *Further education and training certificates* | | | |
| 4 | Further education and training band | School/College/Training certificates<br>Mix of units from all | |
| 3 | | School/College/Training certificates<br>Mix of units from all | |
| 2 | | School/College/Training certificates<br>Mix of units from all | |
| *General education and training certificates* | | | |
| 1 | General education and training band | Senior phase | ABET Level 4 |
| | | Intermediate phase | ABET Level 3 |
| | | Foundation phase | ABET Level 2 |
| | | Pre-school | ABET Level 1 |

*Figure 9.2* Proposed structure for an NQF

| *Locations of learning for units and qualifications* | | |
|---|---|---|
| Tertiary/Research/Professional institutions | | |
| Tertiary/Research/Professional institutions | | |
| Universities/Technikons/Colleges/Private and Professional Institutions/ Workplace etc. | | |
| Universities/Technikons/Colleges/Private and Professional Institutions/Workplace etc. | | |
| *Locations of learning for units and qualifications* | | |
| Formal high schools<br><br>Private/State schools | Technical/Community/Police<br><br>Nursing/Private colleges | RDP and labour market schemes/Industry/Training boards/Unions/Workplace etc. |
| *Locations of learning for units and qualifications* | | |
| Formal schools (urban/rural/farm/special) | Occupation or work-based training/RDP and labour market schemes/Upliftment programmes/Community programmes | NGOs/Churches/Night schools/ABET programmes/Private providers/Industry training boards/Unions/Workplace etc. |

171

good deal of the process, as it coloured how spokespersons put forward points of view, debated them, held back from debating them, endorsed or disagreed with them. It may be useful to give a few examples here.

Representatives from the business community were there either because they were nominated individuals believed to be sufficiently or particularly knowledgeable and experienced and able to make an appropriate and responsible contribution; or they were the official education and training people of an organised business grouping; or their organisation was perceived to be either a leader in terms of education and training or a significant player in terms of size and/or the make-up of their workforce or even because of the skills profile and needs of that workforce. These people contributed opinions that may well have been personal but carried weight, or had been previously agreed in caucus. They may also have been convinced that they would be able to persuade those they represented to endorse the opinions they expressed in committee.

Those representing existing (pre-1994) government departments or government institutions of education and/or training tended to express views that defended the status quo; indicated how 'slight' was the change being suggested; spoke in a personal capacity often with the knowledge that complex and, I dare say, heated debate would take place within the staff of those same existing structures. They were views which became increasingly territorial as the debate indicated that radical policy recommendations were likely to follow.

Those representing trade union groupings, and other ANC-related groupings, contributed a great deal in the early stages of the NTB process. This position was usually not documented (or not tabled), but as ideas and proposals firmed, their representatives needed to refer more frequently to their constituency for approval of either the content, or the process, or tactics to be adopted in the process. When consensus had finally been reached, many of them became active in drafting the final documentation.

Thus there was, in the NTB process and, I would be inclined to believe, in other wide groupings and current broadly-based processes, a developing use of terms such as 'mandated' or 'not mandated' views, decisions, agreements.

It appears that when spokespersons represent clearly defined constituencies the movement towards consensus becomes more problematic and the need for internal advocacy increases. There seems little doubt however, that the fact that there was a wide distribution of stakeholders considerably enhanced, not only the content of discussion, but particularly the process. On the other hand, the fact that some processes – such as that of the NTB – changed shape, changed the framework in which they functioned, meant that certain key stakeholder constituencies were not represented, or not adequately represented. An example of this was the formal, general education component – the representatives of the teaching profession in particular

– who were not drawn in to the early stages of the process. They tended to be involved only in the discussions taking place in education *per se* and not in the broader form of debate. This is probably due to the fact that the NTB enquiry moved from 'training' to 'vocational education and training' to 'education and training'.

In my view, an extremely important aspect of the change processes was that the views put forward by every participating group or constituency were given weight and serious consideration. The input was assessed, and incorporated if agreement was reached on the basis of its merit. The representativeness of the process was in no way artificial and there was a high quality of 'listening' in the entire process.

### Group processes towards documentation

This applies to both the separate groups' own work and the integrated groupings.

Figure 9.3 demonstrates what the process followed here, as a generalisation, appears to have been.

### Interpersonal processes

While it may sound trite or even sentimental, a major factor in moving towards consensus was that areas of trust, degrees of trust, high levels of deep personal respect were built up during this process. It is not over-dramatising the situation to say that influential individuals who had seen themselves as being in opposition to each other, as representing all that was worst/most dangerous/most evil(!) in their point of view, were found to have very substantial viewpoints in common. There was, in the process and in many of the groupings, a strong sense of concern for the good of all the people of the country and a surprising degree of shared values, even while yet remaining within differing political and economic ideologies. This trust is proving of great value in the present situation but, perhaps inevitably, is also coming under some strain as we move into new political realities and the change from being in opposition to being in government (and vice versa), places new pressures and expectations on individuals and groups.

It is my conviction that this trust-building grew from the passionate commitment of many participants and an intellectual rigour applied to, not only each other's, but one's own standpoint. This was not an exercise to please the participants – it was seen as being a life and death matter for the nation. Hence the crucial second stage in the change process – after the identification of the pressures – the clear shared vision. That this was shared in the task teams and working committees was evident. Failing in adequate advocacy of options and the concepts they represented is more evident in hindsight.

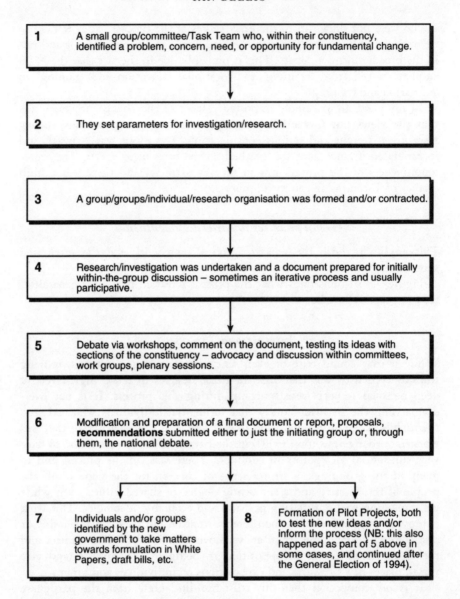

*Figure 9.3* Processes towards documentation

## *The role of language*

This issue is not simply one of being able to speak clearly in a commonly understood language, it raises a number of other issues:

- How does one ensure a common understanding of the debate and of the documentation when (as English was the language used in the process) the medium of communication was, for many, their second or even third language?
- How does one make use of terms or concepts that have historical or intellectual or ideological baggage?
- How does one use terms or concepts that may be acceptable to some, important to others, suspect to yet others and unintelligible to still other groups?
- How does one select terms that have a less emotive impact?
- Can one select a range of terms, as a tactic, to work with 'problematic' concepts so that the important notion or issue is not lost because of the misconceptions or negative experience associated with them?

A few of the areas of discussion where terms needed full explanation were:

1   To emphasise the strategy as a *qualifications* framework was challenged as over-emphasising the qualification *per se*, thus exacerbating an already dangerous emphasis in the country on the 'paper chase'. It became necessary to stress that the enhancement of *learning* was to be the focus, bringing about a further shift away from teaching as being the central issue. Such an emphasis on learning was confirmed in the insistence that certification be the recognition of learning achievement in terms of agreed outcomes.

2   Some in the process, this writer included, would have wanted to speak of an integrated *system* for education and training, whereas the majority – and especially the representatives of the (then) government's education departments – were only willing to speak of an integrated *approach*. The term 'approach' may mean no more than an agreed set of basic values and/or principles. The term 'system' implies structuring towards a greater integratedness – or 'seamlessness' as it was often described. In retrospect, the agreement reached on 'approach' rather than 'system' could be leading to more separateness than was widely intended.

3   There was a great deal of debate around the notion of *competence*. Understanding of the concept and related methodologies for curriculum or course design and development, that were grounded in experience of very narrow, mechanistic examples, resulted in a rejection of the term in favour of 'outcomes': learning outcomes. A focus on outcomes and on 'skill' as the point of departure for curriculum work proved an

175

uncomfortable challenge to those who viewed curriculum processes as primarily content related. The discussion to use outcomes as related to competence was, and has subsequently proved to be, one clear example of using mould-breaking language.

Within the group I was privileged to facilitate, it was argued that while we should use familiar and acceptable terms wherever they did not do violence to what was being sought, it was also necessary to use 'new' terms and concepts simply to 'break the moulds' of rigid, separateness-inducing ways of thinking, processes of doing, and structures for governing.

## The present situation

These comments are made on the basis of my personal observation. I raise them as they may suggest how certain of the processes may have been better handled and they may provide issues for further discussion or investigation.

Across a fairly broad range of those who will have to put the legislation relating to SAQA and the NQF into effect, there is a marked degree of confusion and even anger, certainly a lack of clarity about 'what this will all mean in practice'. A challenge to advocacy, to iterative processes, to greater inclusiveness?

One can sense a perception, fairly widely held, that the will to change is more developed, is stronger, than a clear knowledge of precisely how to proceed. A challenge to further expression, to richer exemplars, to testing notions in practice before policy options become law? Another challenge to better advocacy? A challenge to think through issues before setting in concrete one particular understanding without alternatives having been given full consideration?

There is a good deal of anxiety regarding the capacity to handle the change financially and in terms of human capacity. There is simply not enough in government coffers to increase spending. There may well be not enough people or enough appropriately skilled people to pilot the change. A challenge to more thorough investigation of the implications (cost and manpower) before consensus is asked for, let alone achieved? This issue of capacity is the third component of the change process, as earlier represented (see Table 9.1).

In short, there is a conviction among some that structures (in this case new structures) are already being formed and brought into operation, while further conceptual exploration and clarification is still needed.

The experience of some who are working on pilot projects as they 'struggle to make it happen', is the realisation that 'this is much more complex than we realised'. Consensus reached too early perhaps?

The general education constituency (other than official departmental representation) was rather belatedly brought into the process. This contributed to a sense of alienation, confusion and even hostility in some sections of this very important constituency.

The higher education constituency appeared, originally, to feel that the NTB investigation had little to do with them as its initial focus was on 'vocational education'. They became increasingly involved, but generally very anxious about developments. There is a view in some quarters, that the universities would seek to dominate discussion around 'qualification' and 'standards'. Such domination would be resisted by professional bodies. It is likely that new relationships between the South African Qualifications Authority (SAQA), professional bodies and the universities will be established.

The college sector within the Further Education and Training Band long felt itself to be neglected and under pressure between a strong general education sector and a strong higher education sector. This latter was receiving a great deal of attention through the National Commission on Higher Education whose work was in progress. There has been no serious government attention to the further education sector. A challenge to a number of aspects of the process? A need to think again and even more clearly, whatever the language used, whatever the structures may be, about the area of vocational education and training? A new Task Group was formed in September 1996 to address the further education sector. This is likely to have major implications for vocational education and training in South Africa.

It is already clear that there is a further loss of capacity to make substantial progress because so many of the early participants are now in government jobs or in provincial or national parliamentary seats.

There has been a shift from the issues-based commitment of all in the problem identification, policy-option formulation, and even the policy and legislation phases of the change, to the career-building exploitation of the planning, pilot-project and implementation phases. There is a clear challenge to keep the level of debate on 'issue and concept and principle' active and vigorous.

As this chapter is being written there is some evidence that we are seeing a drifting apart of the education and training sectors. To some extent this is inevitable as the government's Departments of Education and Labour (previously Manpower) retain certain territories of activity that will tend to reinforce this development.

The South African Qualifications Authority (SAQA) has now come into being and as its work begins, there will be increasing interaction with those bodies and organisations who are striving to work towards the objectives of the NQF as stated in the legislation:

- to create a national framework for learning achievements
- to facilitate access to and mobility within education and training
- to enhance the quality of education and training

IAN BELLIS

# References

African National Congress (ANC) (1994) *A Policy Framework for Education and Training*, Johannesburg.
Education Renewal Strategy (ERS) (1992) *Education Renewal Strategy*, Pretoria.
Human Sciences Research Council (HSRC) (1994) *Ways of Seeing the National Qualifications Framework*, Pretoria.
National Education Policy Investigation (NEPI) (1992) *National Education Policy Investigation Report*, Cape Town.
National Institute for Community Education (NICE) (1995) *A Framework for the Provision of Adult Basic and Further Education and Training*, Johannesburg.
National Training Strategy Initiative (NTSI) (1994) *National Training Strategy Initiative Document*, Johannesburg.
National Training Strategy Initiative: Committee 2 (1993) *A Proposal for the Integrated National Approach to Education and Training*, Johannesburg.
Porter, Robert W. (1995) *Knowledge Utilization and the Process of Policy Formation: Towards a Framework for Africa*, SARA, HHRAA and USAID, Africa Bureau.

# INDEX

# INDEX

National Skill Competition (Taiwan) 77
National Trades Union Congress (NTUC) (Singapore) 94, 97–8
National Training Board (NTB) (South Africa) 160, 161, 165, 172–3; Committee 2 165–9
National Training Strategy (South Africa) 159, 161, 168–9
National Wages Council (Singapore) 94
need for change: recognition of 11
negotiation period: Taiwan 79, 81
neo-classical theory 91
neo-liberalism 1, 10
networks 12; informal 151
New Apprenticeship Scheme (NAS) 90–1
New Job Training Scheme (NJTS) 31–2
New Right 64
New Training Initiative 29
New Zealand 5
Ng, Sek-hong 86
Niven, S. 3
non-governmental organisations (NGOs) 164

O'Donnell, R. 46
O'Dwyer, L. 57
OECD 49, 52, 55–7
office clerks' training-ordinance 114–18, 119–20
O'Neill, M. 63
O'Neill, Tip 144
on-the-job training see industry-based training
open learning 160
Osborne, D. 21
O'Sullivan, D. 49
O'Toole, A. 47–8
outcomes: learning 175–6
overlapping consensus 11–12
Ozga, J. 8

Pang, Eng Fong 90
PAP 95–6, 97
parameters: determination of 115
parents 140, 141, 142; conservative parents group 145–6
participation 5–10
participative democracy 10, 18

partnership: achieving consensus 14–16; discourse in Ireland 53–5; Scotland 20, 21–4
Partnership 2000 47–8, 65
Pateman, C. 8
Paterson, L. 20, 31
Pempel, T.J. 92
periphery and core 91–2
Perry, P.J.C. 25
Pignatelli, F. 21, 23
pilot projects 17–18, 136, 151–2
planned action 162, 166
planning 154; multilevel 127–8
pluralist society 11–12
policy-makers 172; US 141, 142, 145–6
policy processes 162–3, 166
political parties 34, 131
political will 164–9
politics 163; communication and 16
Pollock, J. 30
polytechnics 124, 129–30, 133–4
portability 169
Porter, R.W. 163
post-compulsory education participation rate 56, 129
Post-Leaving Certificate Courses (PLCs) 56, 61–2
pressure for change 162, 165, 166
Primary School Leaving Examination (PSLE) 89
principals 132
principles for integration of education and training 166–9
prior learning: recognition of 168
Private Industry Councils (PICs) 32
private schools–public schools resource gap 83–4
private sector 32–3; see also employers/business community
proactive approach to change 3
problems 163
process owners 131–3, 135–6; see also stakeholders
Productivity and Standards Board (PSB) 89
professionals 82–3
Programme for Competitiveness and Work (PCW) 44, 45, 46–7
Programme for Economic and Social Progress (PESP) 43–4, 45
Programme for National Recovery (PNR) 43–4, 45

INDEX